WATCHING THE PATH OF YOUR FEET

WATCHING THE PATH
OF YOUR FEET

Michael C. Sharrett

Thank you, Linda, for sharing our 31st anniversary with us, and the wonderful cake! May the Lord fill your heart with grace,
Mike

Metokos Press
Narrows, VA 24124

Written permission must be secured from the publisher, Metokos Press, to use or reproduce any part of this book, except for brief quotation in critical reviews or articles. Contact Metokos Press at 211 Main Street, Suite 108, Narrows, VA 24124.

Unless otherwise indicated, Scripture quotations are from the NEW AMERICAN STANDARD BIBLE®. Copyright © 1960, 1962, 1963, 1968, 1971, 1972, 1975, 1977, 1995 by The Lockman Foundation. Used by permission.

Scripture quotations are also taken from The Holy Bible, English Standard Version, copyright 2001 by Crossway Bibles, a division of Good News Publishers. Used by permission. All rights reserved.

Published by Metokos Press, Inc., committed to providing materials easily accessible to the average reader while at the same time presenting biblical truth from within the framework of biblical and confessional churches of Reformed and Presbyterian heritage. Visit us on the web at *www.metokospress.com.*

Cover design by Chip Evans, Walker-Atlanta, Atlanta, GA.

Printed in the United States by Lightning Source, LaVergne, TN.

ISBN 978-0-9786955-0-7

Dedicated to my wife Janice, and our three children Mike, Luke and Laura, and to David H. Sharrett, Jr., my nephew, who gave the ultimate sacrifice of his life in combat defending my freedom, January 16, 2008.

Preface

My first work, *Watching Over the Heart*, originally included a section called The Heart's Stumbling Blocks. A study on the spiritual care of the heart seemed incomplete without addressing the many causes of stumbling repeatedly specified in Proverbs. Believing that such an addition would make that work too lengthy, I dropped it from that effort and expanded it into this second book, in effect making this a companion piece to the first.

Part 1 of this book examines some of Proverbs' fundamental teachings on wisdom. Part 2 explores the major causes of stumbling addressed in Proverbs.

Acknowledgements

I am thankful for the enthusiastic support of my friends Beth and Dowell Stackpole, whose prayers and financial gifts made this work possible. I remain gratefully indebted to my friendship with Dr. Samuel T. Logan, whose example and encouragement inspire me to press on.

Contents

Foreword

It was once said of Jonathan Edwards that he was "the Mount Everest of theologians."

Why would such a claim be made?

In my opinion, and I do share this perspective on Edwards, it was because he, more than any other human writer, probed the depths of what it means to be a Christian and provided both solid biblical theological exegesis for his conclusions and extraordinarily valuable applications of his conclusions.

Basically, in his remarkable work, "Treatise on Religious Affections," Edwards demonstrated (from both Scripture and human experience) that human identity rests not just in reason (we are not merely what we thing) and not just in emotion (we are not merely what we feel), but in <u>the affections of the heart</u>.

Those "affections of the heart" include both reason and emotion but dramatically transcend both - in this case, one plus one equals one hundred!

The affections of the heart are simply, to use biblical language, the "seeking first" impulses of the heart (Matthew 6:33). Most fundamentally, every human being IS what he or she "seeks first." And this means that the affections of the heart are, in and of themselves, neither good nor bad. It is not the fact of "seeking first" which defines a person as a

Christian; it is the content of what is sought that defines the Christian.

Two brief quotations from Edwards point up some crucial ingredients in how this works.

1) "Holy affections are not heat without light; but evermore arise from some information of the understanding, some spiritual instruction that the mind receives."

2) "No light in the understanding is good which does not produce holy affection in the heart."

There must, in other words, be at least these two ingredients in any presentation which intends to raise "holy affection" in the heart of a reader or listener - solid biblical instruction about the God of Scripture and powerful inducements designed to move the reader/listener to seek first the Kingdom (glory and rule) of the God of Scripture.

It is in the combination of these very two ingredients that Mike Sharrett is so gifted in his presentations of the truths of Scripture. Over and over again, I have heard or read Mike share his understanding of and love for the Triune God of the Bible. And I have always been both <u>instructed</u> and <u>moved</u>.

This is especially true in Mike's present work on Proverbs. In his examination of that book, he takes us into the very depths of the human heart, from which all kinds of "seeking first" tendencies emerge. He teaches us exceptionally well what this part of God's word reveals to us about indwelling sin's deceit and self-reliance. He then explores, with powerful insight, what the book of Proverbs says about the means of grace which God has provided to deal with the continuing tendency, even in regenerate hearts, to "seek" contrary to what we have professed.

The ultimate expression of those means of grace - now

truly AMAZING grace - is in the person and work of Jesus Christ, a biblical fact which Mike makes abundantly clear.

But making the facts clear is only the starting point . . . both for Jonathan Edwards and for Mike Sharrett. What really matters is that Jesus - His honor and His worthiness - be relished by the sinner. And this is clearly the ultimate goal of the present book.

We seek to live lives of faithfulness not in order to get from God but in order to give to God . . . to give to Him what He deserves, our obedience as much as our worship.

This is why the very practical guidance Mike provides in this book is so valuable. He not only helps us to see the insidious nature of many of the spiritual dangers which surround us; he not only helps us to sense the critical importance of handling those dangers biblically; he also provides clear biblical direction for us and motivates us to want that direction, that Christ-honoring direction, to define our very lives.

In my judgment, Jonathan Edwards would have loved this book!

Samuel T. Logan, Jr.
International Director
The World Reformed Fellowship

Introduction

Blissful serenity turned to fear. I began my ascent to the summit of Old Rag Mountain[*] with three fellow Boy Scouts, but for one reason or another, a mile up the mountain, the group dissipated and I found myself alone. Alone on a mountain trail I had never hiked. Alone in a fog growing thicker by the step. Alone as the day grew shorter. The white blaze marks painted on trees to show the trail were lifelines, but halfway to the summit, dense forest yielded to large boulders, over, under, and around which the trail snaked. Thus my focus shifted to the ground, searching for the next blaze mark to guide me through the gray mist. Did this double blaze indicate a switchback to the left or to the right? Beyond the edge of the boulders, for all I knew, I could have plummeted a thousand feet.

Then I came to the cave. Dropping to my knees to peer inside, I noticed the large white letters spray painted on the cave wall:

TURN BACK   DANGER   BEWARE OF SNAKES

Too naïve as a seventh-grader to recognize the work of a prankster, I froze in fearful confusion. Could this really be the trail? Did it circumvent the cave to the side where the ground appeared beaten down? What should I do? I had come too far to turn back. Why in the world did we separate from each other coming up a mountain we'd never hiked? I took my chances on

---

[*] Central Section of the Shenandoah National Park, Virginia

the cave, crawling through with eyes wide open, screaming out loud to try to scare away the snakes. After many wearying mental exercises worrying about stumbling or slipping on the rocks, getting stuck in a narrow crevice, or simply losing my way, I finally arrived at the campground, where, incidentally, one of the scouts was visited by a copperhead during the night.

Why this story about my adolescent trauma? It pictures life. Life is a path we've never walked, and for all our desire for the familiar and the comfort of routine, we still find ourselves on unfamiliar trails. Sometimes it's foggy, confusing, and fearful. Sometimes we feel left by the pack and all alone. Sometimes we get mixed messages—is the cave simply another passageway or are there really snakes?

Oftentimes the path is more dangerous than we're aware. Not until I had hiked the boulder-laden summit of Old Rag in the daylight did I realize how many places I could have walked right off the edge of the mountain in the fog. If this is life, what are we to do?

The Bible says, "Watch the path of your feet and all your ways will be established. Do not turn to the right nor to the left; turn your foot from evil" (Prov. 4:26-27). Here Solomon is exhorting us to live intentionally, carefully, eyes wide open, and alert for trouble. "The naïve believes everything, but the sensible man considers his steps" (Prov. 14:15). There is no justification for strolling aimlessly through this world. It's simply too dangerous, according to the God who sees and knows all. Rather, a sense of urgency permeates the wisdom of Proverbs.

"Watch the path of your feet" is simultaneously a command, a warning, and a promise. We are commanded because God knows what life is like and He knows how to instruct us to negotiate it carefully. The warning arises because He loves us and wants our safe passage, yet we're prone to wander on our own terms. "Every man's way is right in his own eyes, but the Lord weighs the hearts" (Prov. 21:2). Ignorance is not bliss. "The waywardness of the naïve will kill them, and the complacency of fools will destroy them" (Prov. 1:32). Thankfully, God promises we will not get sidetracked or stumble if we follow the path of life: "all your ways will be established" (Prov. 4:26b).

These truths are what the wise person knows and the fool ignores. While if you are a wise person you will "direct your heart in the way" (Prov. 23:19), and live by the promise, "You will walk in your way securely, and your foot will not stumble" (Prov. 3:23), tragically "the way of the wicked is like darkness; they do not know over what they stumble" (Prov. 4:19). Indeed, the adulteress "does not ponder the path of life; her ways are unstable, she does not know it" (Prov. 5:6).

Does that strike you as pathetic? Some people stumble because they aren't looking, or they refuse to admit the possibility of snares, or they are naïve about true danger. Life is fraught with peril, and the sooner we know it, the better. "A man who wanders from the way of understanding will rest in the assembly of the dead" (Prov. 21:16).

How do we avoid stumbling? "Do not enter the path of the wicked, and do not proceed in the way of evil men. Avoid it, do not pass by it; turn away from it and pass on" (Prov. 4:14-15). You need to know what to avoid. "Let your eyes look directly ahead, and let your gaze be fixed straight in front of you" (Prov. 4:25). You need the wisdom of God's Word. "The teaching of the wise is a fountain of life, to turn aside from the snares of death" (Prov. 13:14). It will never deceive you. "I have directed you in the way of wisdom; I have led you in upright paths" (Prov. 4:11).

*What do we need to know about the path?**

If you have ever driven a road for the first time, you appreciate the yellow highway signs that mark sharp directional changes and curves in the road. A study of Proverbs reveals similar road signs along the path of life that tell us what it is like. Think of the following words as individual road signs that mark the distinct features of the path.

1. Contrasts

Proverbs studies two paths: the path of uprightness or the

---

* See Chapter 4 in *Watching Over the Heart* for further discussion.

righteous, also called "the paths of life" (Prov. 2:19), compared with the path of darkness, the way of evil, whose "tracks lead to the dead" (Prov. 2:18).

"So you will walk in the way of good men, and keep to the paths of the righteous" (Prov. 2:20). "Discretion will guard you, understanding will watch over you, to deliver you from the way of evil . . . from those who leave the paths of uprightness, to walk in the ways of darkness . . . whose paths are crooked" (Prov. 2:11-15).

2. Irony

The path that *seems* right is the wrong one. "All the ways of a man are clean in his own sight, but the Lord weighs the motives" (Prov. 16:2).

"Every man's way is right in his own eyes, but the Lord weighs the hearts" (Prov. 21:2). We innately cut ourselves slack; we hide our motives from ourselves. "There is a kind who is pure in his own eyes, yet is not washed from his filthiness" (Prov. 30:12) .

3. Safety

You can never hurt yourself on the correct path. It is trustworthy because obedience will never lead you to a place of danger for your soul. "In the way of righteousness is life, and in its pathway there is no death" (Prov. 12:28).

4. Instruction

By its nature the path requires constant interpretation and information from the Lord of the path. "He will die for lack of instruction, and in the greatness of his folly he will go astray" (Prov. 5:23). "He is on the path of life who heeds instruction, but he who ignores reproof goes astray" (Prov. 10:17). "Do not let your heart turn aside to her ways, do not stray into her paths" (Prov. 7:25).

5. Self-validation

"But the path of the righteous is like the dawn, that shines brighter and brighter until the full day" (Prov. 4:18). This verse gives great hope to those on the path, slugging it out with sin and detractors. It seems to promise that the longer we are faithful to the path, the clearer we will see what is right and how distasteful evil really is. When we start the walk of life, we love our sin too much. We feel too comfortable with the darkness; righteousness may feel odd while sin seems normal. But as we keep on it, the path—like the sun, increasingly illuminating the earth—appears less and less fuzzy and more and more clear. We long for the light of God's revelation so we won't stumble in the darkness.

God's law may not make sense at first, but as we continue to walk in its light, according to Psalm 19, it is "restoring the soul . . . making wise the simple . . . rejoicing the heart . . . enlightening the eyes . . . [and being] more desirable than gold . . . sweeter than honey and the drippings of the honeycomb."

6. Providence

God says your job is to stay on the path, while His job is to make it straight. He will take you where He wants you to be. He will never lead His own astray. He will fulfill His good plans for His children. "The mind of man plans his way, but the Lord directs his steps" (Prov. 16:9) .

"Commit your works to the Lord, and your plans will be established" (Prov. 16:3). "Trust in the Lord with all your heart, and do not lean on your own understanding. In all your ways acknowledge Him, and He will make your paths straight" (Prov. 3:5-6).

God gives us abundantly sufficient help for the path of life. We don't have to wander alone in fear. His markers are trustworthy because He is trustworthy. We have His Son Jesus Christ as our constant companion and guide. As our pioneer, He has walked the path safely and righteously before us. In His Word, we find the wisdom we need to order our steps in the blessedness of righteousness.

On a singles retreat years ago, I met a Christian man who shared with me a story that illustrates what these truths are teaching. We discovered a mutual love of basketball, exchanging stories of playing in high school. He shared how hard he worked to be a starter his senior year; yet with a large crop of juniors coming along, the coach chose to play them instead. That left the senior with a choice. He could become bitter about this providence, or respond in faith, with the love of Christ, acknowledging the Lord was in control.

The coach's young son attended all the practices. My friend, who made the team but did not play much or scrimmage with the starters, chose to pour his off-court time into the coach's son, helping him develop his basketball skills, rather than mope during practice about not getting things his way. It was hard not to play with the starters, but he clearly believed the thing God wanted him to do was to spend time with the coach's son. His senior season ended pretty much a disaster, from a basketball perspective. But he stayed on the path, he didn't lean on his own understanding, he trusted the Lord.

Years later as a businessman, his work took him to a manufacturing plant in China. Apparently many of these plants have outside basketball courts for recreation, and the Chinese workers take their hoops very seriously. After he completed his work in the plant, the local workers invited him out to their court for a game. Hundreds of onlookers framed the court. He played. Yes, he played the best basketball of his life, lights out. He said the plant laborers were in awe of him, as if he were Michael Jordan. God returned to him a serendipitous moment of basketball glory, not what he was seeking at all, but a kind of "straight path" for his selfless sacrifice in high school. God did not have to give him that experience, but we can be certain it was His pleasure to do so. That "Michael Jordan day" may seem like a small thing to you, but for my friend it was God's way of acknowledging the man's trust in the Lord during a tough time. It was as much God's good plan as was his ministry to the coach's son.

.

PART 1

FUNDAMENTALS ON WISDOM

The Beginning of Wisdom

The fear of the Lord is the beginning of wisdom. (Prov. 9:10)

During World War II my grandfather served as an American officer with the Royal Air Force. He developed a friendship with a British officer, Jack Wire, with whom he was in bombardment school. One day an instructor began to teach about the specific intricacies of dismantling a certain bomb fuse. When the instructor explained that a screw was turned one direction to dismantle it, Jack Wire raised his hand to interrupt. "Sir, I believe you need to turn the screw the opposite direction." Not to be upstaged, the instructor said indignantly, "If you're so smart why don't you come up here and show us all how to do it." So Jack Wire went to the bomb and proceeded to dismantle the bomb down to the minutest detail. With stunned awe the instructor queried, "How do you know so much about this bomb?" Jack replied, "I invented it."

Who invented life? God. Who knows best how life works? The inventor, God. Where does God tell us how life works? Generally in His Word, more specifically in the Wisdom Literature, and most particularly in Proverbs.

Wisdom is insight into the created order, the fixed, eternal socioreligious order that God created and upholds, according to Old Testament scholar Bruce Waltke. Wisdom gives us understanding of the relationship of man to man, man to the world, and man to God. That's very helpful, because life often feels like there are lots of bombs inside and outside us waiting to explode: pressure to perform, expectations of others, the need to find meaningful purpose, the challenge of managing anger, crippling fears, demoralizing disappointments, rejection, lust, and many other strong pulls on the heart. We spend a lot of emotional energy trying to defuse these things. But there's a problem. Our instincts for dismantling life's bombs are flawed and untrustworthy. If we don't start with the right understanding and equipment, we'll lack the insight and tools necessary to avoid blowing up ourselves and others around us.

Where do we find out how the world is wired? "The fear of the Lord is the beginning of wisdom" (Prov. 9:10), echoing "the fear of the Lord is the beginning of knowledge" (Prov. 1:7). The word "beginning" means a starting point, the first principle, or the indispensable equipment. The beginning of serious bird watching is possession of binoculars. You can't do it without the right equipment. Just as binoculars are essential and indispensable to serious bird watching, so "the fear of the Lord" is the lens without which we will never focus on life accurately. Having "the fear of the Lord" means you see at least four fundamental truths.

One, "the fear of the Lord" sees that God observes every part of your life. "For the ways of a man are before the eyes of the Lord, and He watches all his paths" (Prov. 5:21). "Sheol and Abaddon lie open before the Lord, how much more the hearts of men!" (Prov. 15:11).

This means I am accountable to God. There is no such thing as moral neutrality, there is nothing God doesn't care about, my actions have consequences for eternity, and I can experience the pleasure of knowing that God delights in my obedience.

Two, "the fear of the Lord" sees that wisdom can't save you. It doesn't have all the answers. If all you have is wisdom, you can be streetwise and stay out of trouble, but you can't make yourself righteous by it. Wisdom can't make you right with God. "Who can say, 'I have cleansed my heart, I am pure from my sin'?" (Prov. 20:9). You admit your IQ can do nothing about your guilt before God. It is as if you're stuck in a little house in the middle of the prairie, surrounded by a raging fire. Because there is nowhere to flee, it's only a matter of time until you are overwhelmed by the flames. If you decide to take a shower and clean yourself, is that going to save you from the flames? You can engage in all manner of religious activities, but will they shield you from the inferno? If you decide to do tons of good things for other people in the house, will that keep you from the fire? If you offer all your money to God, will that save you from the flames? If you make yourself the most educated person in the world, that still avails nothing against the impending inferno. "The fear of the Lord" knows there is no human activity that saves or delivers you from the guilt of sin.

On the contrary, salvation comes through belief in a promise God makes in the gospel: "I promise to accept you based on what My Son has accomplished." Jesus was consumed by the flames to make a safe way out to the Father. Jesus delivers you from the wrath due your sins by His being consumed by it. "For Christ also died for sins once for all, the just for the unjust, so that He might bring us to God . . . " (1 Peter 3:18). The fear of the Lord moves a believer's heart from terror and helplessness to freedom, joy, and delight. God saves you at the cost of His own son. "And He Himself bore our sins in His body on the cross, so that we might die to sin and live to righteousness; for by His wounds you were healed" (1 Peter 2:24).

Three, "the fear of the Lord" sees or admits that, to our own detriment, we fear ourselves. We respect too much our own view of things. Our interpretation of life makes perfectly good sense to us. We think we know the right way, but it is wrong. "There is a way which seems right to a man, but its end is the way of death" (Prov. 14:12).

Katharine Hepburn wrote in her book, *All About Me*, "I don't know if there is an Almighty. We have to take matters into our own hands and use plain old common sense." That is exactly what God says not to do. Like the bombardment instructor, we are bound to turn the screw the wrong way. Despite the fact that it *seems* right to us, "He who trusts in his own heart is a fool" (Prov. 28:26).

Foolishness is our biggest problem. We think the screw to defuse life's bombs turns one way; in reality, it turns the opposite. Therefore, Scripture warns, "Do not lean on your own understanding. . . . Do not be wise in your own eyes" (Prov. 3:5, 7). The answer is not within, contrary to popular opinion. We have an internal moral compass that consistently points to self-justification. If you don't believe it, consider that in your relational difficulties, you nearly always lay the bulk of the blame on the other person. Or consider how quick you are to criticize other drivers on the road, when in fact you do the same dumb things they do. Or think about how slow you are to admit fault.

Four, "the fear of the Lord" sees that God knows best how to dismantle life's bombs. Therefore, we need the inventor to reorient us to the way things work. You thought you were the instructor—no one needed to teach you—but now you humbly bow to the wisdom of the true Teacher. We need God's wisdom. "The fear of the Lord" is a reorienting of our lives to the Lord—His mind, ways, paths, and truth.

It is a matter of life and death. "He who finds [wisdom] finds life" (Prov. 8:35). "The teaching of the wise is a fountain of life, to turn aside from the snares of death" (Prov. 13:14). Therefore, "the fear of the Lord" is a fundamental reorientation of our lives from self to God.

The critical question that follows is, Why would we do that? Proverbs seeks to answer that question in terms of the benefits of "the fear of the Lord." Here are three benefits:

1. "The fear of the Lord" liberates you.

"Indeed they (parents' teaching and instruction) are a graceful wreath to your head, and ornaments about your neck" (Prov. 1:9). "Keep sound wisdom . . . . [It] will be life to the soul, and adornment to your neck" (Prov. 3:21-22). There are several aspects of life in which "the fear of the Lord" liberates you:

Guidance. The adornment around the neck is symbolic of guidance. It's always there as a reminder. Did you ever need to get someplace to visit someone, and then realize you had no idea where to go? You're not free until you have reliable directions. Without true guidance you are a slave to ignorance. Those who are free take their orders from God, know they are not their own, and resist being autonomous decision-makers. They are children of the King who live by His Word. "When you walk about, they (your parents' teaching, representing God's teaching) will guide you" (Prov. 6:22).

Victory. The wreath on the head symbolizes the victor's crown, the winner who masters life. If we fear the Lord we are free from all of life's traps for success. As long as we do all things for God's glory, we can't fail. That's why I explain to my children that getting good grades in school should be motivated by glorifying God.

Beauty. Don't we all have some internal idea of what makes us attractive? You're pursuing a picture of yourself that you believe makes you appealing to others. I spoke with a woman once who admitted her frustration that men apparently didn't find her appealing. She said, "I don't get it. I'm smart, I have an excellent career, I try to stay in shape . . . why aren't men falling for me?" Maybe it's a mercy of God. Don't you want others to like you for more than these things? Why not a "gentle and quiet spirit, which is precious in the sight of God?" (1 Peter 3:4). If a man doesn't want you for your spiritual beauty, do you really want him?

How does "the fear of the Lord" make you attractive? It is both a standard and a motive for moral beauty. As a standard, "the fear of the Lord" is equated with righteousness. Godly people are attractive, as a rule. I know that others can be rebuked by the guilt they feel in the presence of a person seeking to do the right thing. But as a rule, people are drawn to the inner beauty of a godly spirit.

"When a man's ways are pleasing to the Lord, He makes even his enemies to be at peace with him" (Prov. 16:7). Why is that? A godly spirit tends to produce other-centeredness in people, because God is graciously other-concerned. All Americans look with favor on those who sacrificed to save others on 9/11 or who risked their own welfare to help people ravaged by Hurricane Katrina. Whoever criticized Mother Teresa? Such a heart of mercy, self-sacrifice, and caring is so close to God's.

I was speaking with a college student once who explained

to me that she really wanted to be married and have a family. I asked her what kind of man she wanted to marry. "A man who loves Jesus more than anything else." To her, that kind of man would be most attractive. Her desire for that kind of man is also evidence that she herself fears the Lord.

"The fear of the Lord" is also a motive for godly living. When my kids and wife found a $20 bill in a parking lot at a shopping center, my wife didn't assume "finders keepers, losers weepers" (although the kids and I did!). She knew it wasn't ours. So she waited by the car in the event the woman who apparently dropped it while getting out of her car would be back looking for it. Predictably, a few minutes later she returned and started looking on the ground. My wife asked her what she was seeking. "A $20 bill," was the answer. She gave her the money.

Why would we not just take the money and run? We know we are accountable to a higher authority, answering to God and not our own passion for self-indulgence. There are few things uglier than someone living for himself. Do you want people who manage your money to answer to the God of the universe? Do you want medical personnel who care for you to be ultimately motivated by their wealth or God's glory? Do you want the pilot of your jet to follow strict rules of safety while landing the plane in a thunderstorm, or would you rather he be a maverick with something to prove?

2. "The fear of the Lord" protects you.

Charles Bridges says in his commentary on Proverbs that "the fear of the Lord" is a child bending himself humbly and carefully to his father's will. Why would a child do that? Because the child believes the father is so good. Can you hurt yourself obeying your passions and impulses? Quite easily. Can you ever hurt yourself obeying God? No, never! "But he who sins against me [Lady Wisdom] injures himself; all those who hate me love death" (Prov. 8:36). "The fear of the Lord prolongs life, but the years of the wicked will be shortened" (Prov. 10:27). Why? Because by "the fear of the Lord" you avoid dangerous ways of living. It's dangerous to live as a thief; you end up in jail if you live as a thug. You will never contract venereal disease by keeping God's standards for sex. People who are living contrary to God's ways have anxiety, wondering when they are going to get caught. When will I be found out? When will I slip up? Those who tell lies always have to wonder when they will forget which lies they've told to whom. "By the fear of the Lord one keeps away from evil" (Prov. 16:6) because He'll never lead you into it! David's prayer in Psalm 25:4-7 captures the spirit of this well:

> *Make me know Your ways, O LORD;*
> *Teach me Your paths.*
> *Lead me in Your truth and teach me,*
> *For You are the God of my salvation;*
> *For You I wait all the day.*
> *Remember, O LORD, Your compassion and Your lovingkindnesses,*
> *For they have been from of old.*
> *Do not remember the sins of my youth or my transgressions;*
> *According to Your lovingkindness remember me,*
> *For Your goodness' sake, O LORD.*

"The fear of the Lord leads to life, so that one may sleep satisfied, untouched by evil" (Prov. 19:23). If you're a drug dealer or if you traffic in illegal things, your company is likely to be people who will kill you when they have no need of you. The fear of the Lord protects a society, as well. "When the wicked rise, men hide themselves" (Prov. 28:28). "When the righteous increase the people rejoice, but when a wicked man rules, people groan" (Prov. 29:2).

What, therefore, is the greatest protection for your soul? True thinking about God, that is, "the fear of the Lord." Here's ultimately how this works. What is the most dangerous thing in life? Wrong ideas about God. If your views of God are skewed, everything else is bound to be wrong. Notice how God rebukes Israel in Psalm 50:21: "You thought that I was just like you." Or Psalm 54:3: "They have not set God before them." When we have deficient views of God, nothing will be seen in its most accurate light.

Suppose someone gave you an opportunity to seek a buried

treasure. They promised you a brief, ten-second look at a treasure map. That was to be your only help in finding the treasure. Would you look at it in a dark room, or would you bother to turn on the lights?

"The fear of the Lord" leads us to Jesus Christ, the light of the world. You know His light has shown in your heart when you realize God is too holy for you to know without some kind of covering or protection. Jesus is that refuge and shield. By faith in Him, we are assured of the cleansing of His blood, and the covering of His righteousness. God is the Father who does not spare His Son to bring us to Himself! When you see God clearly, you want Him more than anything. If you don't want God more than anything, you're still seeing a god of your own fashioning.

3. "The fear of the Lord" satisfies you.

The popular band from San Diego, Switchfoot, sang, "We were meant to live for so much more." That is a helpful challenge to any of us who are seeking our earthly peace in the things of this life, on our terms instead of God's. Lady Wisdom sang a similar song. The Prologue (Proverbs 1-9) is an infomercial on the need for, sufficiency of, and satisfaction of wisdom. The writer is very good at marketing. Look what he promises about wisdom:

> *For the Lord gives wisdom; from His mouth come knowledge and understanding. He stores up sound wisdom for the upright; He is a shield to those who walk in integrity, guarding the paths of justice, and he preserves the way of His godly ones. Then you will discern righteousness and justice and equity and every good course. For wisdom will enter your heart, and knowledge will be pleasant to your soul; discretion will guard you, understanding will watch over you. (Prov. 2:6-11)*

> *How blessed is the man who finds wisdom, and the man who gains understanding. For its profit is better than the profit of silver, and its gain than fine gold. She is more precious than jewels; and nothing you desire compares*

with her. Long life is in her right hand; in her left hand are riches and honor. Her ways are pleasant ways, and all her paths are peace. She is a tree of life to those who take hold of her, and happy are all who hold her fast. (Prov. 3:13-18)

Do not forsake her and she will guard you; love her and she will watch over you . . . . prize her and she will exalt you; she will honor you if you embrace her. She will place on your head a garland of grace. (Prov. 4:6-9)

So critical is the need to bow before God in "the fear of the Lord" that some verses seem to promise more than we can imagine. "The fear of the Lord is a fountain of life" (Prov. 14:27). The image of the fountain conveys abundance, constancy, freshness, and satisfaction, which go deep to the soul. Do you believe the comparison, "Better is a little with the fear of the Lord, than great treasure and turmoil with it?" (Prov. 15:16).

Media mogul Ted Turner got part of it right. He was asked what it is like to be so wealthy and influential. He said, "Life's a bag. You throw all this stuff in it, and when you look inside, it's empty." He's right; life is indeed an empty bag without "the fear of the Lord." Turner's reflection would appear to echo the famous rich man who was asked what he would trade for all his riches? He answered, "one happy marriage." Both men's answers reveal how elusive true satisfaction is without "the fear of the Lord." "The reward of humility and the fear of the Lord are riches, honor and life" (Prov. 22:4).

Conventional wisdom says happiness depends on getting what you want. But that always leaves us at risk. We can't control our circumstances. That's why we're anxious or fearful of failing to get what we want. We can't control other people, so we're frustrated and manipulative and self-protective. Your soul is too large to be satisfied with these things without "the fear of the Lord" in it. If you know Christ, you have all the honor and wealth a person could desire. In Him, you are adopted into God's family and blessed with every spiritual blessing in the heavenly places.

17

If you belong to Jesus by faith, you can be sure He is seeking to strip you of every shred of self-reliance in order to teach you "the fear of the Lord." Consider several scenarios where self-reliance may be exposing your need of "the fear of the Lord." What are you like when you don't get what you want? What do you want when you don't want the Lord? What would you be like if God gave you over to your deepest wishes? What do you do when you're alone? What are you hiding from your closest friends? You know "the fear of the Lord" is functional in your heart when Proverbs 3:32 rings true: "For the devious are an abomination to the Lord; but He is intimate with the upright." Nothing could be better than intimacy with God.

The Way of Wisdom

Wisdom shouts in the street, she lifts her voice in the square; at the head of the noisy streets she cries out; at the entrance of the gates in the city, she utters her sayings. (Prov. 1:20-21)

A few years ago I bet my kids that our dog Maggie was, in the final analysis, most loyal to me because I was the man of the house. To prove it, I invented a game. We'd sit at opposite ends of our long hallway with Maggie sitting in the middle between us. Then we'd simultaneously call her to come to us. She'd invariably come toward one of us, upon which the entreating would intensify from the opposite end of the hallway, *"Come here, girl,"* while the pleading continued from where she had first headed, *"Staaaaaay, Maggie."* (The rule was that you couldn't touch her.) You get the idea. We called this "loyalty." You may be thinking this was really cruel, but don't worry. Maggie understood it was just a game, and we trusted that she understood it served as a great illustration for life.

We all live among competing voices for our hearts' affections or loyalties. This is what Proverbs portrays as the crisis of wisdom: to whom will you listen? After some introductory remarks, the writer says, "Wisdom shouts in the street, she lifts her voice in the square; at the head of the noisy streets she cries out; at the entrance of the gates in the city, she utters her sayings" (Prov. 1:20-21). Then again we hear her, "Does not wisdom call, and understanding lift up her voice? On top of the heights beside the way, where the paths, meet she takes her stand . . . . " (Prov. 8:1-2). Finally, at the conclusion of the Prologue, "[Wisdom] has sent out her maidens, she calls from the tops of the heights of the city: 'Whoever is naïve, let him turn in here!'" (Prov. 9:3-4).

However, the crisis is not simply, will you listen to Lady Wisdom, but will you also recognize and refuse the invitation of the antagonist, Dame Folly? "The woman of folly is boisterous, she is naïve and knows nothing. She sits at the doorway of her house, on a seat by the high places of the city, calling to those who pass by, who are making their paths straight: 'Whoever is naïve, let him turn in here . . . .'" (Prov. 9:13-16).

When you hear two voices, both appealing to folks trying to do what is right, both offering things needed, both winsomely persuasive, how do you tell them apart? You need wisdom.

The genre of wisdom

Compare wisdom laid out in the Bible with other parts of God's revelation. It's not the law, distinguishing right from wrong. Nor is it promises per se. It is not history, reporting God's saving acts for His people. Wisdom is knowing what to do when the rules don't apply. For example, it's *not* a wisdom issue whether you have an affair with your secretary (that is a law issue); it *is* a wisdom issue how much time you spend with her. It's *not* a matter of law exactly how much you spend on entertainment, landscaping, or clothes, but it *is* a wisdom issue how much disposable income you set aside for a rainy day need.

Wisdom doesn't come in the form of do's and don'ts, but rather in the form of a father (representing both parents) speaking to his son (representing all children). Chapters 2-7 of Proverbs each begin with the phrase, "My son . . ." or "Hear, O sons . . ."

Wisdom seeks to apply three things: knowledge (what I know), character (what I am), and skill (what I do). To help me understand the way things are, Proverbs uses two main words for wisdom. The first word means insight or discernment. The root carries the idea of noticing or making distinctions. For example, those who judge diving events or figure skating have an eye trained to see the finer nuances of performance that go unnoticed by the novice. I couldn't tell a good triple toe loop from an average one to save my life. Wisdom is the power to look at life and to make distinctions. And you can't afford to be a novice where life is dangerous. For example, you should use care in the friends you choose ("If sinners entice you, do not consent" Prov. 1:10.), how much you should say in any situation ("When there are many words, transgression is unavoidable" Prov. 10:19.), how long you should stay ("Let your foot rarely be in your neighbor's house, or he will become weary of you and hate you" Prov. 25:17.), how intensely your desires rule your life ("For wisdom is better than jewels; and all desirable things cannot compare with her" Prov. 8:11.), or whether or not you pursue the good life on God's terms or your own ("Long life is in her [Lady Wisdom's] right hand; in her left hand are riches and honor" Prov. 3:16).

The second word for wisdom connotes the power to form plans realistically. How effective will your plans be? It depends. Do you go to a picnic planning to start the fire with wet matches? Won't work, will it? Why not? Your plans don't comport with the way things work. Effective plans must conform to the way God has wired His world and to the principles in His Word. Proverbs (the idea of the book is comparisons) are aphorisms, coined sayings, or pithy statements expressing truths about life or the way the creation is put together. They are generalizations because they state principles that can't be turned into absolutes. They normally can't stand on their own. Like many buoys marking the channel to port, you need lots of proverbs to chart the safe way, as well as wisdom to know in which situation any particular proverb applies. For example, as soon as you rejoice that *"It is the blessing of the Lord that makes rich"* (Prov. 10:22), you need to balance that with the warning, "Riches do not profit in the day of wrath, but righteousness delivers from death" (Prov. 11:4).

While God is infrequently mentioned, the Proverbs assume a theocentric worldview. Because God made the world, owns it, rules it, and cares for it, He established the laws by which it works. He wants life to work, but only the way He prescribes. Therefore, there is no moral neutrality, nor are there purely objective moral observers. You are either moving toward wisdom or away from it toward foolishness.

We can't move toward foolishness without serious consequences. "'So they [who refuse God's wisdom] shall eat of the fruit of their own way, and be satiated with their own devices'" (Prov. 1:31).

The Crisis of Wisdom

To whom will you listen? We see lots of contrasts in Proverbs: the way of life versus the way of death; the walk of the wise versus the walk of the foolish; "the fear of the Lord" versus . . . do you know the opposite? The opposite of "the fear of the Lord," which is the beginning of wisdom, is being true to your self. Conventional wisdom says, only you can decide for yourself what you will be, or what matters to you. When the day is over, what trumps everything is self-respect.

Rosie O'Donnell was interviewed years ago in *Parade* magazine, specifically concerning the little boy she adopted. When asked what she considered the most important thing she could teach her son, she said, "Self-respect. If you have self-respect, you can make difficult decisions about your life and understand the need to take care of yourself and be true to your beliefs." That is exactly what "the fear of the Lord" is not.

What do we call a society where everyone is true to his or her beliefs? Chaos or anarchy. One year, after we purchased back-to-school supplies for our kids, I noticed a divider page in one of the notebooks. It was produced by Reebok.

I am strong because I believe in myself.
If my life were a movie, I'd be the writer, director and star.
I know who I am and what I can do.
It doesn't matter what I look like, where I live or who my friends are.
What matters is the confidence that I carry within.
I am in charge.
This is exactly where I belong.
I know exactly where I'm going and how to get there.
Because this is my planet.

I confess this got my attention, so I called the marketing department at Reebok to ask a few questions. "Who comes up with this stuff?" "We pull from different sources." "Do you believe this—are you serious?" Silence. Sounding a bit perturbed, "Yes, we're trying to build children's self-esteem and to keep them off drugs. . . . Why?" "Because if everyone lived this way we'd have moral chaos." That was the end of the conversation.

I don't doubt for a second that the marketing folks at Reebok were sincerely trying to do good. There's some truth in what they're saying. They're in the mainstream of popular culture. But is this kind of thinking really helpful or really dangerous? You be the judge. Consider that Israel is roundly condemned by God in Judges when "every man did what was right in his own eyes" (Judges 17:6).

Conventional wisdom believes the answer is within. Trust your heart. You see this in almost every movie or television program made for popular appeal today. It clearly shows up in the view of children. If given the right opportunity they will do the right thing, because they are capable, autonomous moral agents. Popular culture thus reveals society's view of human nature: people are basically good. If we accept humanistic presuppositions about the nature of humanity, we fail the first crisis of wisdom: do not listen to yourself.

When my son was in the third grade in public school, the parents attended a presentation in the auditorium called "Heroes." We sat through a lengthy program during which every child in the third grade announced from the stage who was a hero. Heroes included bus drivers, teachers, garbage collectors, sports figures, politicians. Well, the list went on and on. The idea was very clear. *Everyone* is a hero. Then came the punch line: *I am my hero.* This is simply nonsense because the definition of a hero is someone you look up to and want to be like. If I'm my own hero, the concept is meaningless.

Children need instruction in life. Again and again we are all exhorted to get wisdom, and to do whatever it takes to do so. "Acquire wisdom! Acquire understanding!" (Prov. 4:5). Hence, Proverbs often takes on the tone a parent adopts while teaching his teenager to drive. You have a running commentary on every move! "Wait, stop, look, speed up, move over, slow down, be careful!" You've got this dangerous, powerful machine and you're never *not* at risk! Life is like a machine, full of risks. We may want to think we have the answer within and we can figure things out on our own, but God says that attitude will hurt you more than anything.

Conventional wisdom says that goodness is bound up in the heart of a child. What does God say? "Foolishness is bound up in the heart of a child" (Prov. 22:15). Take the attractive cover off a baseball and you see that the core is bound with string. If you could see your heart the way it really is, you'd see it bound with cords of foolishness, the commitment to do things your way. But here's the irony: it takes wisdom to see that.

Fools think they're wise; wise people know they've got foolishness residing within. "Fools despise wisdom and instruction" (Prov. 1:7). "The way of a fool is right in his own eyes" (Prov. 12:15). The fool's creed is, don't tell me what to do or how to live. "All the ways of a man are clean in his own sight" (Prov. 16:2). "There is a kind who is pure in his own eyes, yet is not washed from his filthiness" (Prov. 30:12). "Every man's way is right in his own eyes" (Prov. 21:2). Notice how Lady Wisdom rebukes the fool: "Because I called and you refused, I stretched out my hand and no one paid attention; and you neglected all my counsel, and did not want my reproof; I will also laugh at your calamity; I will mock when your dread comes" (Prov. 1:24-26).

What is the reason we're this way? "The foolishness of man ruins his way, and his heart rages against the Lord" (Prov. 19:3). The result? "There is a way which seems right to a man, but its end is the way of death" (Prov. 14:12). Translated: my internal moral compass always points to self-justification. I'm prone to dismiss myself; I'm a persistent defender of my own cause. When I sit as judge over my moral inclinations, I am very lenient. This does not mean that reason, intellect, or inquiry is bad. They are faulty because they are tainted by sin. Because of our inherited sin nature from Adam and Eve, we are all predisposed to minimize our guilt, think too highly of ourselves, pass the buck, avert blame, and insist our way is best. "He who trusts in his own heart is a fool" (Prov. 28:26).

24

The Grammar of Wisdom

For the LORD gives wisdom; from His mouth come knowledge and understanding. (Prov. 2:6)

Almost monthly, I receive an email from a wealthy foreigner offering me a share in his or her millions of dollars. Funny how the stories are basically all the same, cleverly complete with the misspellings and typos we'd expect from a foreigner. Because of some governmental problem, all their millions need refuge in America with someone as good and trustworthy as me. Usually the appeal has some connection to God, as well. I am free to use all this money for my church, ministry, or whatever, "in the sacred name of Jesus." Here's an excerpt from one:

> *It is also my wish that this deal be handled as quietly as possible without any leakage to the press. If you agree to act as fund manager to me, I will release the money to you if you meet the requirements . . . . Your commission will be six million USD . . . you shall be entitled to 40% of the after tax returns for the first two years of managing my money . . . .*
>
> *Best regards,*
> *Mr. Idris E. Idemen*

So you may be wondering why I am not a billionaire by now. Is it because I'm so perfectly content with what I already have? Not a chance. It's because of wisdom. These emails are a complete hoax by evil people trying to get my money or personal information. Not falling for this doesn't make me a genius. When scams like this work, in most cases it is because people are as greedy as they are gullible. But once you apply the *grammar* of wisdom, it's not hard to see right through the hoax. You and I do this in one way or another all the time.

What is the *grammar* of wisdom? Just as language study starts with its grammar—spelling, diction, syntax, subject-verb agreement, etc.—and math study starts with its "grammar"— the addition and multiplication tables—so wisdom is founded on its "grammar"—those basic principles ordering life according to God's design. Without knowing and applying these, it's impossible to grow in wisdom. There are at least five important grammar principles delineated in Proverbs:

1. Actions have consequences.

That seems pretty obvious, but nonetheless this is a truth that must be learned. To be wise, you need the grace to learn from your experiences so that you know the implications of cause and effect. For example, years ago someone persuaded me to use very expensive synthetic motor oil in my car. So I shelled out the cash, changed the oil myself, and stood back from the car to admire how smart I was to prolong the life of my car with synthetic oil. Yes, I stood back, only to notice this expanding black pool of something under my car—under the oil pan—you know, the place where you drain the old oil by unscrewing the plug, which you replace *before* putting in all that very expensive synthetic oil. That is, unless you like seeing it seep onto your driveway. Actions have consequences. I never again made that mistake, believe me.

Some actions are self-preserving. "He who keeps the commandment keeps his soul, but he who is careless of conduct will die" (Prov. 19:16). If you play carelessly with fire, or guns, or chemicals, or fast dirt bikes, or whatever, sooner or later you are going to hurt yourself. Who is surprised that Evel Knievel supposedly had broken almost every bone in his body? "He who returns evil for good, evil will not depart from his house" (Prov. 17:13). If you are in the habit of being mean to people for no good reason, especially when you spitefully rebuff their good intentions, you'll find yourself living in a den of controversy, tension, and agitation. "Can a man take fire in his bosom and his clothes not be burned?"

(Prov. 6:27). If you think you can get away with sex outside God's good parameters, you don't understand the grammar of sexuality.

Some consequences are just helpful to happy, productive living. "Hatred stirs up strife, but love covers all transgressions" (Prov. 10:12). God is saying that, as a rule, hatred doesn't help relationships; it always hurts them. Why do you need to win all the disputes you have with others? Why do we suddenly dislike a friend when he decides to risk the relationship by challenging us on an area of sin in our lives?

Consider an almost comical illustration of the consequential cost of productivity. *"Where no oxen are, the manger is clean, but much revenue comes by the strength of the ox"* (Prov. 14:4). It's messy and hard to produce wealth, but isn't it worth it? If you want the crops produced by strong oxen, you need to feed them. If you feed them you will have some cleaning up to do.

Parents, are you teaching your children early in life that actions have consequences? If you get caught lying, you lose credibility and can hardly ever be trusted again. If you abuse a privilege, it may be taken away. That's true with dart guns or drivers' licenses. Better to have learned the hard way, than not to have learned at all. Trust the nature of things instead of appearances. When I was in the fifth grade. I climbed a tree in a neighbor's yard, went out on a limb, and jumped into this huge pile of soft, fluffy leaves. I estimated that a leaf pile so high and soft-looking was sure to give me a gentle landing. I went right through the pile to the ground and chipped my tooth on my knee!

To be sure, you don't have to make mistakes to learn about consequences. You can learn from the mistakes of others if you're wise. And when we're slow learners, it's good to know that God is more patient with us than we are with ourselves. He is a good father, a teacher, and a helper, abounding in patience and understanding.

2. Get instruction.

If you want to be wise, you need to be in a posture to learn, to receive aid, to admit you don't have all the answers. Come on men, why don't we typically want to stop and ask for directions? We're prideful; we don't want to concede that we didn't know what we were doing. We don't want to look like the incompetent folk God already knows we are. We have forgotten that "the fear of the Lord is the instruction for wisdom" (Prov. 15:33), or that you "will die for lack of instruction" (Prov. 5:23), or that we should "heed instruction and be wise" (Prov. 8:33).

Prov. 21:16 seems to indicate that we never really arrive; instruction is a lifelong pursuit. "A man who wanders from the way of understanding will rest in the assembly of the dead." What would lead you off the path of understanding? Thinking you had no more to learn. The truth is that none of us is ever a know-it-all or beyond needing teaching. Proverbs reveals at least three primary forms of instruction:

Teaching. Teaching is instruction from God's Word about God and all that is necessary for godliness in His world. The primary source for this is parents: "Hear, O sons, the instruction of a father, and give attention that you may gain understanding" (Prov. 4:1). "Observe the commandment of your father and do not forsake the teaching of your mother" (Prov. 6:20). If you don't believe in innate foolishness, just ask yourself how ready you are to seek, listen to, and cherish the instruction of your parents, assuming they are following after the Lord. Your parents represent God's authority to you; therefore, when they ask you to do something, it's not because they said so, it's because God says so.

Counsel. "Where there is no guidance, the people fall, but in abundance of counselors there is victory" (Prov. 11:14). "Oil and perfume make the heart glad, so a man's counsel is sweet to his friend" (Prov. 27:9). "Without consultation, plans are frustrated, but with many counselors they succeed" (Prov. 15:22).

Reproofs/discipline. This is instruction we need when we have erred or picked the wrong way to live. "A fool rejects his father's discipline, but he who regards reproof is sensible" (Prov. 15:5). "Through insolence comes nothing but strife, but wisdom is with those who receive counsel" (Prov. 13:10). "He is on the path of

28

life who heeds instruction, but he who ignores reproof goes astray" (Prov. 10:17). "He who hates reproof is stupid" (Prov. 12:1).

Proverbs challenges all of us to resist telling people what they want to hear. "He who rebukes a man will afterward find more favor than he who flatters with the tongue" (Prov. 28:23). Parents must use reproof to teach their children that they can't always get their own way. "The rod and reproof give wisdom, but a child who gets his own way brings shame to his mother" (Prov. 29:15).

3. Listen.

This might seem pretty basic, so why does Proverbs make such a big deal about listening? Apparently we aren't so good at it. Maybe that's explained by our innate tendency to think we already know what to do. Let's break down listening this way:

The principle. Listening is a gift of God. "The hearing ear and seeing eye, the Lord has made both of them" (Prov. 20:12). "Listen to counsel and accept discipline, that you may be wise the rest of your days" (Prov. 19:20). We interpret life both through the eye and the ear.

The warning. "A wise man will hear and increase in learning, and a man of understanding will acquire wise counsel" (Prov. 1:5). There's a difference between merely hearing and true listening; listening is a means to the greater goal of understanding. You have not heard someone until you understand what he or she means.

The heart of listening. "Incline your ear and hear the words of the wise, and apply your mind to my knowledge" (Prov. 22:17). "Make your ear attentive to wisdom, incline your heart to understanding" (Prov. 2:2). If we could picture listening with the body, it would look like one hand on the ear and one hand opening the heart.

The result. "Blessed is the man who listens to me" (Prov. 8:34). "But he who listens to me shall live securely" (Prov. 1:33).

When listening breaks down. "He who gives an answer before he hears, it is folly and shame to him" (Prov. 18:13). Give others the privilege of completing their thoughts aloud.

Some situations don't require us to say everything we're thinking. "A fool does not delight in understanding, but only in revealing his own mind" (Prov. 18:2). Realize you have more to learn than you know, and people don't care how much you know. James 1:19 should be considered a clear New Testament summary of these principles. "This you know, my beloved brethren. But let every one be quick to hear, slow to speak and slow to anger."

4. Make comparisons.

Proverbs is full of comparisons, inviting the use of observation. Would you *really* rather have this than that? Think through the consequences; take time to connect the dots. Do you realize the cost beyond the price tag? Have you judiciously weighed the costs and requirements of one choice over another?

Three areas that come up frequently include relationships, "It is better to live in a desert land than with a contentious and vexing woman" (Prov. 21:19); material welfare, "Better is a little with the fear of the Lord than great treasure and turmoil with it" (Prov. 15:16) and "Better is a little with righteousness than great income with injustice" (Prov. 16:8); and character, "What is desirable in a man is his kindness; and it is better to be a poor man than a liar" (Prov. 19:22). The reason we may not be so quick to believe these is that we aren't thinking through our choices.

Implicit in the skill of making comparisons is the ability to observe carefully. "I passed by the field of the sluggard, and by the vineyard of the man lacking sense; And behold, it was completely overgrown with thistles, its surface was covered with nettles, and its stone wall was broken down. When I saw, I reflected upon it; I looked, and received instruction. 'A little sleep, a little slumber, a little folding of the hands to rest,' Then your poverty will come as a robber and your want like an armed man" (Prov. 24:30-34).

It isn't enough just to see things. To grow in wisdom

requires reflection, study, and the receiving of instruction. We even hear the ditty sung by the sluggard. But tragically, the result of excessive hand-folding and sleep is being robbed unawares.

5. See the holy irony.

What do I mean by this? Proverbs tells us that many aspects of life don't work they way we might assume they should. Ironically, in God's economy (i.e., His way of ordering things), the results are not what we expect from a human point of view. In other words, common sense isn't always trustworthy.

Consider some life examples where things work the opposite from how we might intuitively respond. You're in the kitchen, a grease fire breaks out, and so you naturally throw water on it from the sink. Good idea? No, grease fires spread worse with water. But, how would you know *unless* someone told you? A lightning storm rolls in while you're golfing so you head for the obvious safe natural cover, a huge tree. Good idea? No, it's the worst place to be, *if* that lightning strikes a tree and runs down the trunk to the ground. You're having fun in the ocean when you realize you're being taken out to sea in a rip current. Your instincts immediately prompt you to swim against it as hard as you can, straight back to shore. Right move? Wrong. The way to survive a rip tide is to let it take you out to sea (though it feels counterproductive and dangerous) or to swim across it, parallel to the shore. Again, you would have to know that from a source other than your instincts.

Wisdom learns not always to trust your instincts, not to trust the initial appearance of matters. This tends to be important in areas that have potential to exert power over us.

Treasures. "There is one who scatters, yet increases all the more, and there is one who withholds what is justly due, and yet it results only in want" (Prov. 11:24). See the irony? The person who is generous (scatters) doesn't lose, but gains. The person who hoards (withholds), thinking he will preserve what he has, actually ends up with less.

"One who is gracious to a poor man lends to the Lord, and

he will repay him for his good deed" (Prov. 19:17). How ironic that when you lend to someone who has nothing you actually give to the One who has everything. "He who gives to the poor will never want, but he who shuts his eyes will have many curses" (Prov. 28:27).

Time. "The way of the lazy is as a hedge of thorns, but the path of the upright is a highway" (Prov. 15:19). The lazy person thinks he's taking the easy way, but it really is the toughest.

Ourselves. Fools think they're wise; wise people know they have foolishness. "A man's pride will bring him low, but a humble spirit will obtain honor" (Prov. 29:23). Our pride motivates us to be honored and exalted because we want recognition, credit, or attention, yet it does the opposite.

Human relationships. "A gentle answer turns away wrath, but a harsh word stirs up anger" (Prov. 15:1). "A flattering mouth works ruin" (Prov. 26:28). When we flatter, we think we're building up, not tearing down. "The fear of man brings a snare" (Prov. 29:25). While we think we're free when people like us, the effect is that we become slaves to their opinions.

Divine relationship. "Riches do not profit in the day of wrath, but righteousness delivers from death" (Prov. 11:4). Look, that man is well off, so he must be morally acceptable to God. He has a lot of stuff; he's secure. Wrong, because he can't buy the most important thing in life, the shield that protects in the face of the judgment of God. Riches give us a false feeling of comfort or being at ease. If my stomach is full and there's money for the next year, I must be in good shape for eternity.

Holy irony is at the heart of our redemption. God the Creator becomes man the created. The king becomes a pauper. The one who had no servants was called Master. The one with no formal education, they called Teacher. He had no medicines, yet He was the Great Physician. He had no army, yet kings feared Him. With no military victories, He conquered the world. The Prince of Peace goes to war! He loved the unlovely; He clothed the filthy in His own righteous garments.

32

Jesus wins by losing; He gives life out of His death. Out of humiliation comes exaltation. The just died for the unjust. The holy one takes on sin. The cross, an ugly instrument for execution, becomes the symbol for the whole world to be reconciled to God. In His love he hated sin enough to be punished for it.

The Enemy of Wisdom

For the waywardness of the naïve will kill them, and the complacency of fools will destroy them. (Prov. 1:32)

All was still and quiet one July night at our new home in the country. Around 2 a.m. I awoke to our Labrador retriever barking in the kitchen. It sounded more earnest than normal dog grumpiness, so I went downstairs to determine the problem. I flipped on the light, only to find the dog barking at a snake on the floor of the kitchen, a long snake, a snake which at 2 a.m. looked a whole lot like a poisonous copperhead. So I did what any red-blooded male would do, I ran to the stairs and called for my wife, "Honey, get down here, there's a snake in the kitchen!"

She arrived, surveyed the scene, and suggested I get something from the basement to deal with it. So I ran downstairs and returned with a hard-toothed garden rake. "That won't do—get something else." So I found a spade shovel, the kind with the flat edge like a guillotine. I knelt on the island in the middle of the kitchen, poised above the innocent reptile, and let him have it. I turned to my wife and said, "Could you please take it outside!"

Why the story? Because you too have a snake in your kitchen. The Bible calls it foolishness. Foolishness naturally resides in all our hearts. It's there from the time of our birth. "Foolishness is bound up in the heart of a child" (Prov. 22:15). Unless it is systematically removed through godly discipline, it remains like a snake in your kitchen, an intruder that must be removed.

I know it's alarming, offensive, and humiliating for someone to tell you that foolishness is in your heart. Our hearts resist that: "I'm not foolish!" It was especially humiliating having a snake in my kitchen because guests were staying the night with us. The guests were one of my heroes, a seminary professor, and his family. They woke up because of the commotion. In fact, it was amusing how the mother watched nonchalantly from the kitchen door. When her kids surfaced from the basement, rubbing the sleep from their eyes, and asked what was happening, she said matter-of-factly, "Mr. Sharrett is just killing a snake in the kitchen." They said, "Oh," and went back to bed, in the basement, the basement where the snake obviously had been hiding out since construction of the house.

I know you don't like being told that foolishness is in your heart. It doesn't mean stupidity, it doesn't mean you're unlikable or unsuccessful, or that you don't do lots of helpful things.

There are eight different Hebrew words used for foolishness, and they carry the idea of dull, obstinate, or un-teachable. Foolishness is a technical term in the Bible. The fool is one of four kinds of people Proverbs addresses (the young, the naïve, the wise man, and the fool), and it describes a mental outlook, an attitude toward life.

The irony with our innate foolishness is that even though it is self-destructive, we don't know it's there. It's not like a pimple, blemish, birthmark, or wart we can see; it's like a disease silently infecting our heart. No child ever voluntarily went to his parents and said, "You know, I have innate foolishness in my heart and I want you to discipline me until it's removed. Dad, I'm usually wrong, please correct me and impart all your wisdom to me. Don't spare the rod. Make life hard on me if I need it. Keep spanking me until I really change."

So, there is an undetected foreigner in your heart, and you can't just wake up every morning and say, "Hello snake, wherever you are, where do you want to go today?" Unless it is continuously removed, it remains until you die. Just as every time we entered the house for months after this incident, looking carefully for more snakes (in closets, under furniture), so too we need always to check our hearts for residual foolishness. It's no fun, but it's critical for walking before God in wisdom. It's a matter of life and death. "For the waywardness of the naïve will kill them, and the complacency of fools will destroy them" (Prov. 1:32).

If there is a snake in your kitchen, how will you know it's there? Someone has to bark you awake so you can turn on the light to see it. That's what God does by His Spirit in His Word. He shows us what foolishness looks like, and what to do about it. Let's examine three marks of foolishness.

1. The fool refuses to admit he's a fool.

The fool thinks he's wise; the wise person battles indwelling foolishness. "The way of a fool is right in his own eyes, but a wise man is he who listens to counsel" (Prov. 12:15). "He who trusts in his own heart is a fool" (Prov. 28:26). "Do you see a man wise in his own eyes? There is more hope for a fool than for him" (Prov. 26:12). He is his own sovereign interpreter of reality; he'll make sense out of life without God; no one can tell him what's best for him. "There is a way which seems right to a man, but its end is the way of death" (Prov. 16:25).

Do parents generally know what's best for their children? In a greater way, God knows what's best for us because He made us. But, "A fool rejects his father's discipline" (Prov. 15:5). We see this today with designer religions. We want God on our own terms. If it suits me and works for me, it can't be wrong.

When confronted with his error, the fool won't learn; therefore, the fool refuses correction or rebuke. "Fools despise wisdom and instruction" (Prov. 1:7). "A fool does not delight in understanding, but only in revealing his own mind" (Prov. 18:2). "A rebuke goes deeper into one who has understanding, than a hundred blows into a fool" (Prov. 17:10).

Why are we this way? Foolishness is actually a symptom of a greater problem. The organic reason for all this is our hostility toward God. "The foolishness of man ruins his way, and his heart rages against the Lord" (Prov. 19:3). "He who walks in his uprightness fears the Lord, but he who is devious in his ways despises him" (Prov. 14:2).

37

Do people really know it's that way? No, foolishness deceives us from seeing our innermost self. "The foolishness of fools is deceit" (Prov. 14:8).

In our heart of hearts we know God is at the center of all things, and we don't like it. We know He's holding us accountable and we despise it. We want to be autonomous, free thinkers. It's back to the Garden of Eden and the first sin; Satan tempts Adam and Eve with a simple proposition, "Although God has said this, why don't you decide for yourself. You be the judge of what's best for you." You don't believe that it is this way? Do you constantly consult with God in a spirit of humble submission for all you do? Are you naturally defensive, disliking being challenged by others, proven wrong or ignorant? Only our innate foolishness can account for this.

Let me share an example of this from my own life. Years ago I went to Atlanta on Amtrak for a meeting. A friend picked me up at the train station and a day later, after we spent time at his home, he took me to the meeting place at a hotel near the airport. When it was time to get back to the train station for the trip home, I asked the bellhop at the hotel for directions. I thought I knew the way, after looking at a map, but just to confirm my hunch I asked anyway. I told him what I was planning to do, and he explained that I couldn't get there that way. "You have to take the subway way north of the station, change trains and come back to Amtrak," he corrected. I thought that sounded complicated and stupid; it couldn't possibly be so difficult, so I chose my way. What does he know anyway, I wondered condescendingly.

Well, guess who really knew best how to get to the train station? The bellhop. It was his business to know. So I went my way ("The way of a fool is right in his own eyes."), got off the subway where it made sense to me, and walked up to street level, where I saw businesses, buildings, very few people, but no Amtrak. So I started asking passers-by, none of whom knew where Amtrak was. Finally I found someone who knew, and he said it was two miles that way, pointing down the street. Now I'm wondering whether I'm going to be late for the train. So I start running, in street shoes, with two heavy suitcases. What a fool!

Does life feel like you're running down the street with two heavy bags, not really sure where you're going? Can you admit that perhaps part of the problem is you—you're plagued with innate foolishness? This is a hard word indeed. Are you hearing it, or are you still in denial?

If you're sensing the desperation of the depravity of your own heart, you need to know something wonderful. God cares about you. He sees you running with two heavy suitcases, having made a mess of matters, and his heart breaks for you. He'll carry your burden, He'll give you direction, and He'll forgive and change you. How?

You must admit to God, yes, I am at war with you, I can't win that war, you *are* God after all, and I can't cleanse myself to make everything right. When you admit that, God says, "I'll go to war for you." In Jesus Christ, God came to earth to win a war for fools that they know they can't win themselves. What our foolishness deserves is capital punishment; yet Jesus died on the cross in our place as the criminals we are. What our foolishness requires of us is perfect wisdom and righteousness; Jesus lived that acceptable life in order to credit us with His moral perfection. In Christ, God makes us beautiful in His eyes. But there's more. He also promises to give us new hearts. Lady Wisdom cries out to all, "How long, O naïve ones, will you love being simple-minded? And scoffers delight themselves in scoffing, and fools hate knowledge? Turn to my reproof, behold, I will pour out my spirit on you, I will make my words known to you" (Prov. 1:22-23). God pours out His spirit that we might be delivered from foolishness.

2.   The fool is ruled by his emotions.

"The complacency of fools will destroy them" (Prov. 1:32). The idea behind complacency is a feeling of false security. The fool reasons, If nothing has happened to me in spite of what I've done, it must be all right. If it feels good, do it. As long as I don't get caught, it must be fine.

I've always tried to stay in shape to keep my body working well. But a few years ago I reached a point where I didn't feel like exercising very much. However, I did it anyway, on principle. If I

39

exercised only when I felt like it, it wouldn't happen much. If I was obedient to God only when I felt like it, it might not happen as much. If students waited until they felt like studying, they wouldn't get as much done. Many of you may not feel like going to work, but principle (if you don't work you don't eat) trumps any given feeling. Don't wait until you feel like praying to start praying; don't wait until you feel like showing mercy to the poor to do so; don't wait until you feel like giving cheerfully to start giving generously.

We all feel lazy, critical, angry, lustful, vindictive, or insecure, but this isn't license to be that way. We must subject our feelings to questions: What am I telling myself that has me feeling this way? What do I believe I need right now to be whole, to feel human? What desires are fueling my feelings?

Wisdom discerns the difference between desire and principle. It knows you shouldn't make major decisions when you're tired, angry, or anxious. Don't let your heart be ruled by your reaction when you don't get what you want, when you feel scorned, defensive, needy, hopeless, and full of self-pity. Ask the Holy Spirit to enable you to let principle win the day.

How can you tell when your emotions rule you?

By the way you talk. "A fool's mouth is his ruin, and his lips are the snare of his soul" (Prov. 18:7).

By your readiness to quarrel. "Keeping away from strife is an honor for a man, but any fool will quarrel" (Prov. 20:3). "A fool always loses his temper, but a wise man holds it back" (Prov. 29:11).

By your response to wisdom. "Do not speak in the hearing of a fool, for he will despise the wisdom of your words" (Prov. 23:9).

By how you handle honor. "Like one who binds a stone in a sling, so is he who gives honor to a fool" (Prov. 26:8).

By your sense of sin's gravity. "Fools mock at sin, but among the upright there is good will" (Prov. 14:9).

Proverbs warns about the consequences of being ruled by your emotions: you will be deemed untrustworthy, "He cuts off his own feet and drinks violence, who sends a message by the hand of a fool" (Prov. 26:6); caution will give way to carelessness, "A wise man is cautious and turns away from evil, but a fool is arrogant and careless" (Prov. 14:16); and you will become enslaved to your foolishness, "Like a dog that returns to its vomit is a fool who repeats his folly" (Prov. 26:11).

3. The fool lives for the now.

Could I have said to the snake in my kitchen, "You're not bothering me right now, you can stay"? Wisdom lives beyond the moment; it thinks, observes, calculates, and considers the end of a matter. If you don't farm with an eye toward the harvest, you end up begging and have nothing (Prov. 20:4), If you spend all your disposable income today you have nothing for your children's inheritance (Prov. 13:22).

Imagine a young lady who stays with a friend and her family at their lake house. The young lady's parents give her $60 for gas and food for the week. When it is time to drive home, she has to ask her parents for more money. Why? Because she spent $45 on a canoe rental. Would it be nice to have a canoe? Sure. It is essential to happiness? No. It can never be essential if you can't afford it. Whatever you need for happiness, God will provide. If He hasn't given it, you don't need it. The fool refuses to live within her means.

The pursuit of sin (self-indulgence now) will blind you to what's important. "The way of the wicked is like darkness; they do not know over what they stumble" (Prov. 4:19). It will distract you from your primary calling, from pursuing the things God wants you to do. "The eyes of a fool are on the ends of the earth" (Prov. 17:24). This verse reminds me of the star of the Honeymooners, Ralph Kramden, played by Jackie Gleason in the 1950s television comedy. Ralph was always seeking some outlandish way to get rich, often risking the security of his job as a bus driver.

Proverbs shows us how the adulteress, and the man caught up with her, both have spiritual nearsightedness. All they see is the pleasure of the moment, with no consideration for the result of their conduct. "For the lips of an adulteress drip honey and smoother than oil is her speech; but in the end she is bitter as wormwood, sharp as a two-edged sword. Her feet go down to death, her steps lay hold of Sheol. She does not ponder the path of life; her ways are unstable, she does not it" (Prov. 5:3-6). How can you be unstable on a path and not know it? You must be intoxicated with something that dulls your God-given sense for what is right, self-preserving, and honorable.

Most of us know how thoroughly true to life this is. We've witnessed highly gifted Christian leaders resign from key posts because of adulterous relationships. What were they thinking? Where in their affections were spouse and children? If you live for the now you've virtually stopped thinking.

We're often blind to the impact of our selfishness on others. When I was in high school, I was in serious competition . . . for the family car. There was only one car for three busy brothers. One day I was so much in the now to go somewhere, and to beat my brother to the car, that I zipped into the garage, hopped in the car, started it, backed out of the garage as quickly as I could, only to learn that I was in such a hurry I forgot to close the car door. Whack, the car door hit the side of the garage and bent all the way around, pointing the opposite direction. That's a clear example of foolish selfishness at the cost of blessing another. Are people in your way to happiness? What are you doing to them? Are you treating them the way you want to be treated?

Proverbs also warns that if you live for now you may be susceptible to unhealthy peer relationships. Some people want to be accepted and valued so desperately they will engage in relationships, whether for fun, adventure, popularity, or thrill, that blind them to the negative effects that bad company may have on their values. If you'll do anything to be liked, you tread on the thin ice of foolishness. "My son, if sinners entice you, do not consent . . . do not walk in the way with them. Keep your feet from their path, for their feet run to evil . . . ." (Prov. 1:10,15-16) "Do not be deceived: 'Bad company corrupts good morals'" (1 Cor. 15:33).

Happily, the Bible tells of one glorious exception to this principle. There is one man who can befriend fools and make them better. His name is Jesus. They called Him the friend of sinners. In Him alone are the wisdom, power, purity, and love to befriend a fool and not be swayed by the fool, but rather, sway and transform the fool to become like Himself. He considered the shame, and decided you were worth it.

PART 2

STUMBLING BLOCKS ON THE PATH

Early one frosty morning I stepped down the wooden stairs outside our back door and nearly broke my back. I slipped on a thin layer of ice that I couldn't see. To protect my wife, I told her immediately and then covered the steps with a towel so my son wouldn't slip on his way into the house from his garage apartment.

That's a picture of one way to understand Proverbs. God wants to keep us from slipping, stumbling or falling over the many areas of life in which we daily tread, where we don't always see the ice. Therefore, He tells us what we need to know about the path and He shows us how easy it is to stumble over good things we use along the path, things like food, emotions, sensuality, time, money, sleep, relationships, and words.

How do we use these in constructive ways? Wisdom answers that question. We now turn our attention to the various topics addressed in Proverbs which can be a cause of stumbling for us.

Blessings and Counterfeits of Sex

Let your fountain be blessed, and rejoice in the wife of your youth. (Prov. 5:18)

Is fire destructive or helpful? It depends on how and where it's used. A fire in the floor of your living room is destructive because it spreads and consumes and becomes an untamed monster that produces only ashes and heartache. Yet a gas fire in the oven, heating food, is helpful because it's contained and regulated, serving a wonderful purpose, producing a blessing: food that is delightful and nourishing. In this text, God says sex is like fire: used in the wrong place, it consumes, destroys, and leaves ashes and heartache. Used in the right place, it produces blessings—something healthful and nourishing.

Now the fire analogy is very obvious to us. Anybody can see that. "Can a man take fire into his bosom, and his clothes not be burned? Or can a man walk on hot coals, and his feet not be scorched?" (Prov. 6:27-28). Fire wasn't made for your coat and it doesn't work for flooring—your feet weren't made to walk on it. But, the fact that sex is potentially destructive may not be so obvious. That's why examining this subject begins with a plea to be open-minded. Bible believers are criticized routinely for being narrow and close-minded about sexual values. We're even accused of misrepresenting Jesus on the issue. Bill O'Reilly interviewed an author who said Christians are homophobic because they don't understand that Jesus was all about love and compassion. That's a fairly narrow way of representing Christians and the Bible, and a close-minded way of representing biblical love.

What do I mean by open-minded? Simply this. You should

be careful how you use something you didn't invent. Be open to ideas beyond what you think is intuitively permissible. Most open-minded people check first with the instruction manual before using a device that is powerful. For example, is it close-minded not to walk on hot coals? Yes and no. No, because you did your research with an open mind to the possibilities, determined that flesh always burns on fire, and so yes, the case is closed.

American pop culture claims open-mindedness regarding sexuality. It embraces a view of sexual expression I would call "pure preference." It's up to you to decide how you should express your sexuality. Isn't that the approach of most sex-education programs in public schools? They claim to be open-minded but have their own limits, to be sure. They don't particularly like biblical values of sex; nor is the "pure preference" approach open to perversions such as rape, bestiality, child molesting, or incest. But you see how quickly the question becomes, Where did those parameters come from? Who determined those limits? Someone has become a close-minded standard giver. Where did anyone get the authority to set those standards?

Again, popular culture *seems* open-minded. If you invented sex, you ought to be free to use it on your own terms. If you did not invent it, would it be wise to know how the inventor says it works best? Only if you want to maximize its use for the purpose it was intended—glory and beauty.

Proverbs assumes a lot of things aren't so obvious to us, especially depending on our age and worldview. That's why Proverbs employs the address of a father leading a son to maturity. The parents, the primary mentors for personal health, look at life and speak candidly about things they didn't invent and that are inherently powerful—words, money, wine, emotions, authority, sexuality. They speak as those informed by the Inventor's perspective: here's how you use these to your greatest benefit. The author has walked down the path, seen the pitfalls, seen the genuine and the counterfeit, and shares the wisdom he has gleaned. He has an insider's word from the Creator, so why wouldn't you earn from him? That's what Solomon does in his Prologue with God's great gift of sex; he contrasts the blessings of sex used God's way with the dangers of counterfeits. How to benefit from the gift and use it safely, therefore, is a wisdom issue. To give us wisdom, Proverbs uses four scenarios, each of which raises a question about our motives concerning sex.

1. What does it reduce you to? (Prov. 6:23-29)

> *For the commandment is a lamp, and the teaching is light; and reproofs for discipline are the way of life, to keep you from the evil woman, from the smooth tongue of the adulteress. Do not desire her beauty in your heart, nor let her capture you with her eyelids. For on account of a harlot one is reduced to a loaf of bread, and an adulteress hunts for the precious life. Can a man take fire in his bosom and his clothes not be burned? Or can a man walk on hot coals, and his feet not be scorched? So is the one who goes in to his neighbor's wife; whoever touches her will not go unpunished.*

Wisdom keeps you from the evil woman (who, by implication, could just as easily be a man) who uses her beauty and words to catch you, both of which inflame the imagination, the seat of lust. If you are ensnared by her beauty, you are reduced to your lusts. You've also reduced beauty to thievery. Her beauty is a gift *from* God *for* her husband.

The Song of Solomon celebrates the delight of a husband and wife in one another's physical beauty. But true beauty is always accompanied by the fear of the Lord. "Charm is deceitful and beauty is vain, but a woman who fears the Lord, she shall be praised" (Prov. 31:30). If all that counts is skin, what are you saying about the value of moral glory? What are you implying about those things that get you through tough times, the things you look for in a relationship after someone uses you and discards you, virtues such as loyalty, honesty, patience, sympathy, faith, and kindness?

The evil woman's words, likewise, are given to her as a gift from God for the edification of others. Instead, she abuses them, using them as bait. If you are caught by them you're reduced to a gullible fool. You're naïve and perhaps insecure, if you need her words to feel good about yourself. You also may be reduced to a slave because her words have defined your needs. She's hunting her prey, reducing you to "a loaf of bread" (Prov. 6:26). When you fall to sexual perversion you will feel empty. If you use pornography, your soul will feel like stale bread. You think you're consuming it, but it also reduces you to its prey—it keeps hunting you, distorting your view of romance, the opposite sex, and real personal intimacy. Proverbs 6:33-35 says you are reduced to a fugitive. Unlike a thief who can make restitution, you fail to see you cannot repay the harm done. See the difference between stealing someone's bread, which you can pay back, and stealing the purity of a marriage bond, which cannot be paid back?

Is there any help in this passage? Yes, verse 23 reminds us that God won't do this to His own. You're precious. To whom? To the God who fashioned you for Himself. You bear his image. He doesn't reduce us, He elevates us! The gospel tells us He paid the price of our salvation, by the death of His own Son, and binds us forever to Himself in that love. God turns slaves into sons. He rebuilds us in His own true human glory by the Holy Spirit. When your greatest sense of personhood is tied to being the Lord's precious one, you won't fall for false suitors.

2. Do you have a consumer mentality? (Prov. 2:16-19)

> *To deliver you from the strange woman, from the adulteress who flatters with her words; that leaves the companion of her youth, and forgets the covenant of her God; For her house sinks down to death, and her tracks lead to the dead; None who go to her return again, nor do they reach the paths of life.*

What's the evidence the evil woman (or man) is a consumer? Two things. First, using words for your own ends, for your benefit and not another's, getting someone to like you, deceiving for selfish purposes, in short, flattery. It's often the case that illicit relationships begin with seemingly innocent conversation that can be nuanced: "You look pretty today; I feel so understood by you; no one really knows this about me but I want you to know: you're really fun to be around; I never met a person like you."

Words are very powerful tools to create attraction. God woos us to Himself through His written Word. God gives us words for ministry, not as a lasso for roping people into our agenda, but as building bricks for lifting them up for a clearer view of God, to encourage one another, to communicate our hearts or dreams, and to create faith. Verse 6:24 says the evil woman's words are *smooth* (literally, slippery), perhaps indicating that, with her, there is nowhere to land your heart for security. You're never certain whether you stand secure in the relationship.

The second piece of evidence the evil woman is a consumer is her covenant breaking. "[She] forgets the covenant of her God" (Prov. 2:17). What is the covenant of her God that she breaks? There are probably three binding realities in her life forming the covenant of her God. First is the covenant law, the seventh commandment, which is given to protect her from self-harms. (Who questions the unspeakable pain and heart-shattering rejection of adultery?) Second is the covenant of grace, by which she has been made a member of the most privileged community on earth. In the covenant, God befriends the unlovable, the unlovely, and the stranger to His holiness. God pledges to us in His covenant to love, save, protect, provide, and be our God. To walk out on that for adultery is treason. It is saying God isn't worth sticking with. It's better to have this momentary sexual adventure than to enjoy everlasting paradise with God. "For her house sinks down to death, and her tracks lead to the dead; none who go to her return again, nor do they reach the paths of life" (Prov. 2:18-19). Third is the marriage covenant. "[She] leaves the companion of her youth" (Prov. 2:17).

The heart of the marriage covenant is companionship: emotional, personal, intellectual, physical, and spiritual oneness. The only way it works is within the bonds of a covenant, by which couples pledge to each other, "I'm going nowhere, I will be with you till death do us part." Without a covenant agreement you never know when your partner will say, "You're no longer serviceable to me so I'm looking for satisfaction in someone else—it's all about me." If you don't believe your selfishness is the greatest threat to your marriage, you may be destroying your marriage companionship. That's one reason verse 18 says this is the way to death. Life is only found in giving ourselves away. When you consume (take without giving) in a relationship you consign it to death.

3. Is this intensity without intimacy? (Prov. 7:6-8, 10, 15, 18-19, 21-22)

> *For at the window of my house I looked out through my lattice, And I saw among the naïve, I discerned among the youths, a young man lacking sense. Passing through the street near her corner; and he takes the way to her house . . . . And behold a woman comes to meet him, dressed as a harlot and cunning of heart. . . . Therefore I have come out to meet you, to seek your presence earnestly, and I have found you. . . . Come, let us drink our fill of love until morning; let us delight ourselves with caresses. For my husband is not at home. . . . With her many persuasions she entices him, with her flattering lips she seduces him. Suddenly he follows her, as an ox goes to slaughter . . . .*

You could call this chapter "anatomy of seduction." What's the problem here? Aside from the obvious fact that there's another person involved, away on a business trip, who has feelings and a heart, all of this would be fine if they were married. There's nothing wrong with their kissing and caressing within the marriage covenant. In sexual encounters of this kind two people are using each other to feel good. No doubt there's plenty of intensity here. But that's a denial that sex is also about personhood. When you have made sex the goal of a relationship you show yourself to be a crass consumer with no heart for relationship. You're no different than an animal.

Also, her heart is closed. She is "cunning of heart" (Prov. 7:10), meaning guarded or closed. That tells us we're not sure of her motives, though she has persuasive excuses. Maybe cunning plays to the adulterer's fears; they both may be afraid of true intimacy and sexual expression with a person with whom they could share their hearts. How could verse 15 be true ("I have come out to meet you") when this bears all the marks of a random encounter?

God's design for human sexuality is intensity with intimacy, or the joy of being known and sharing secrets. Soulmates make the best bedmates. Soulmates share bodies *and* hearts that give, love, sacrifice, and serve. From this definition, do you see one of the problems with pornography? Pornography offers a form of intensity but without intimacy. This kind of intimacy is impossible apart from the gospel. In the gospel, two critical questions for my sense of well-being are answered. Am I safe? Yes, Jesus has freed me from the condemnation of the law. Am I a valued person? Yes, by faith I am united to Christ and God treats me as He does His own Son. Only in that posture will anyone be free to take the risk of being intimate. Only from a posture of being secure in Christ can we experience the pain of love, with its disappointments and failures, without it crushing us.

4. Is this God's pleasure, God's way? (Prov. 5:15-19)

> *Drink water from your own cistern, and fresh water from your own well. Should your springs be dispersed abroad, streams of water in the streets? Let them be yours alone and not for strangers with you. Let your fountain be blessed, and rejoice in the wife of your youth. As a loving hind and a graceful doe, let her breasts satisfy you at all times; be exhilarated always with her love.*

God is no killjoy or prude. Sexual pleasure is God's invention and should be a regular part of the marriage relationship. Paul forbids depriving one another in 1 Corinthians 7:2-5. Sex is a signpost to glory, to the presence of Christ, which is the ultimate pleasure of perfect love—being known and knowing intimately.

We were created for sexual pleasure, but God did not stop there. The greater pleasure is knowing intimately the God of pleasure, Jesus Christ. In Him is the love you're looking for, love that transcends the fear of being exposed. The gospel of Jesus Christ promises total acceptance without shame and condemnation because He went to the ultimate extreme for you—suffering a tortuous death on the cross to cleanse you of sin.

Valiant Companion

An excellent wife, who can find? For her worth
is far above jewels. (Proverbs 31:10)

For several years my wife taught second-graders at a classical Christian school in Texas. For one assignment, she had the children write a paragraph on the subject, "Mom." Here are three samples from her class:

My mom is always looking out for me. I pray for her each night. Her specialty is cooking meals and playing games. She has brown eyes, and smells like roses and violets. I am so happy my mom had me born to believe in Christ. (Victoria)

My mom is married to a man. She has brown hair, green eyes, smooth hands and rough feet. My mom does the laundry and the dishes. Every day she helps us with our homework. Her free time is !napping!! but she loves us and God no matter what I do! (Benjamin)

My mom is so beautiful that her reflection even feels bad. Her favorite hobby is loving me and kissing me. She is so nice. Mom's meals are so good. Our mom loves me so much that she lets me go to school. My mother is the coolest most nice mom in the whole wide world. (David)

We can only trust that these children's affection for their moms will endure their whole lives. One day, these two boys, if they're wise, will ask their mom a very important question. Do you know what that is? Maybe it will be in response to an inquiry such as this, "Son, you've graduated from college and landed a good job—so when are you going to settle down with the right girl?" What question can we hope will follow? "Mom, how do you know what kind of person you should marry?"

It may be that a similar discussion set up the text we are examining. Proverbs 31 is different from the rest of Proverbs in two ways. First, verses 10-31 form an acrostic poem, each stanza starting with the successive letter of the Hebrew alphabet. Second, while the first 30 chapters of Proverbs are written in the form of a father counseling his son, this chapter records a mother speaking to her son, King Lemuel. "What, O my son? And what, O son of my womb? And what, O son of my vows?" (Prov. 31:2). After charging him with carefulness in several key areas of morality (verses 3-9), she turns to a most critical subject for a young man: finding a spouse. Already Proverbs has sanctioned the glory of marriage: "He who finds a wife finds a good thing, and obtains favor from the Lord" (Prov. 18:22). "House and wealth are an inheritance from fathers, but a prudent wife is from the Lord" (Prov. 19:14). "An excellent wife is the crown of her husband, but she who shames him is as rottenness to his bones" (Prov. 12:4).

Those reflections set up the question that frames the text before us: "An excellent wife, who can find?" (Prov. 31:10). It's not that a father can't or shouldn't give an answer to the question, but, perhaps a bit surprisingly, in this case a mother shares her wisdom. Notice it is an evocative question. "An excellent wife, who can find?" The question seems to imply three truths. One, there are various qualities of wives to be found, but it is the *excellent* kind that should be the object of your search. Look at the motivation to try: "For her worth is far above jewels" (Prov. 31:10). Two, it may be hard to find such a woman. Who can *find* her? She's a rare jewel. Ask anyone whether he'd rather be happily married and poor, or wealthy and in a bad marriage. Three, not *everyone* can find her. Well, *who* can? The person who knows what she looks like.

Proverbs 31:10-31 is the portrait of a *valiant* wife, the Hebrew word "denoting competent strength . . . membership in a select group, including a warrior class."* It's a quite comprehensive picture of virtue from A-Z. If you're a wise son, you will want to marry a person like this. If you're a wise daughter, you will want to be like this person. This portrait helps you determine why you do the things you do and what kind of person you are seeking to become.

Everyone in some way develops an image of the type of person he or she wants to be. The initial crisis of wisdom is, Who determines that? In our culture, we see several typical answers.

1. Some say you should decide for yourself. Be yourself. No one can tell you what you should be. Shape your own image; reality is what you make it.

2. Others maintain that it just doesn't matter. Don't think so hard about such matters, just roll with the punches, let life happen, live existentially in the now. It will come to you when it's time.

3. Some people shape their images around the stars— actresses, singers, and athletes—people who have made it big and are successful and therefore popular. So a formula for developing an image is to be like the stars: wear what they wear, talk like they talk, drive what they drive, etc.

4. Some people are so driven for relationship that they will shape their persona according to the person they want to have. I like that guy, and since he likes girls that are such and such, I'm going to be such and such.

The Bible warns that you're going to get hurt if you use any of those methods. Then what is the best starting point? It is "the fear of the Lord." The climax of our Proverbs text is verse 31:30: "Charm is deceitful and beauty is vain, but a woman who fears the Lord, she shall be praised."

What is "the fear of the Lord"? Proverbs 9:10 says "the fear of the Lord is the beginning of wisdom." You can't know God without it, you can't be wise without it. Fear doesn't mean

---

* Waltke, *Proverbs* (Grand Rapids: Eerdmans, 2004), 520

being afraid, as you would cower before your captors or try to avoid them. Rather, it means reverence or awe. Why would you revere the Lord? Because you have a relationship with Him and you know what He is like.

How does that develop? First, as we saw in chapter 1, you admit that you don't fear the right things. In our natural state we fear giving control to God, we fear letting Him in; we want to rule our lives on our own terms, we insist on being our own interpreters of life. Sin blinds us to the terror that should come upon our souls living in rebellion against God. Second, you admit that nothing you do can make you right with God. Third, you receive with humble gratitude the gift of acceptance and perfection from Jesus Christ. Fourth, you love God so much and see Him so clearly that you have both utmost respect and deepest affection for Him. He made you, cares for you, orders your life in a wonderful way, and doesn't count your sins against you. So you fear disappointing or grieving His heart. "The fear of the Lord" deters you from sin and keeps you in a spirit of worship. It draws you to prayer and keeps you humble. It creates thirst for intimacy with God, with what happy result? God-centered living frees you for other-centered living. Because the Lord is on your side, you have nothing to fear, nothing to lose. God's grace in Christ is sweet to your soul.

How does "the fear of the Lord" affect relationships? "The fear of the Lord" functions positively and negatively. Positively, God alone knows what makes relationships work, so you'll submit to His way in your relationships. Negatively, it keeps you from trouble. On the path of life are many dangers, toils and snares, but by "the fear of the Lord" we stay safe.

For example, we meet in Proverbs the adulteress. We see her again and again. She's sexy and sweet. She easily answers a guy's top two criteria for relationship: someone who is fun to be with and is attractive. Well, 31:30 says charm (she's fun to be with) is deceitful, and beauty (she's attractive) is vain. Therefore, you need better criteria. That's the purpose of this portrait in Proverbs 31. Here the ideal is described in quite a bit of detail. These particulars give you the information you need to find a lifelong companion, the heart of the design for

God's marriage. It's a covenant of companionship. When God created Eve uniquely for Adam, He did so to resolve the problem of Adam's loneliness.

How do you recognize the fear of the Lord in a wife?

This portrait reveals at least three themes:

1. She values virtue.

Why does the poem focus on virtue and make such a bold statement at its end against charm and beauty? Well, first, because you may never achieve the status this woman has as a wealthy matron in the upper echelon of society, but you can have her heart. God doesn't ask you to be something physically or materially that you may never be. But, you can ask Him for the power of a virtuous heart. Second, virtue is celebrated probably as a polemic against contemporary cultural norms. The genre of the text is that of Israel's heroic poetry,[*] which recounts the mighty acts of Israel's heroes (1 Sam. 14:48). Here, the hero is the godly wife and her acts. Virtue is extolled over against the praise of women in ancient Near Eastern literature for their physical charms from an erotic point of view. The Greeks praised a spouse who was a quiet homebody with rare engagement with the world outside. Do you see how special this woman is?

Some of you ladies are seeking accomplishment, accolades, or recognition instead of virtue. To be sure, the Proverbs 31 woman is accomplished and praised—but that is not what she seeks. She fears the Lord. She's a champion of applying wisdom to all of life. No matter whether you are a man or a woman, are you developing your character or are you motivated to seek adventure, pleasure, security, ease? Are you trying to marry a spouse who has money? If you work out faithfully to keep your body in shape, are you as diligent to build relationships that keep your soul in shape? Do you guard yourself so no one can get the best of you, or do you seek to give your best in ministry to others? Do you need to wear a look of confidence or a countenance of grace?

---

[*] Waltke, 517

How is her virtue visible? First, she lives outside herself in gracious spirituality. *"Strength and dignity are her clothing"* (Prov. 31:25). The poem addresses all spheres of her life: She blesses her husband, children, maidens, the poor, and those in the community. She doesn't seek to intimidate, keep others at arm's length, or manipulate. You can do this only if you know you have resources to give away, regardless of whether they come back to you. That's grace. God continually gives it. He opens in your heart a well of grace, so that the more you give, the more you get. Second, her virtue is visible by the way she talks. "The teaching of kindness is on her tongue" (Prov. 31:26). Contrast that with the "smooth tongue of the adulteress," who uses words to seduce as she "hunts her prey" (Prov. 6:26).

2. Her husband values her.

"The heart of her husband trusts in her, and he will have no lack of gain. She does him good and not evil all the days of her life" (Prov. 31:11-12). She is a precious treasure to him. Why? First, she has a heart of gold and it's trustworthy. He wants to live in it because she is for him; she does him good and not evil, with tangible results: "he will have no lack of gain." Second, the home she keeps is a place where he wants to live because it's pleasant, cheerful, clean, and gleaming with virtue. Third, her hands evoke his praise because of her industry. She knows how to wisely provide for the moment and has a vision of the future, never giving in to idleness.

Finally, she is what Eve was given to Adam to be, a helper: "She looks well to the ways of her household, and does not eat the bread of idleness" (Prov. 31:27). They live together in mutual blessing. She resists the sin of Eve, who left Adam's side as a companion and became a tempter. Nothing she does should tempt her husband from fulfilling all that God calls him to be.

Let's be honest. This portrait isn't exclusively about one's wife. Brothers, what kind of man are you that she would trust you? Do you seek her welfare? Does she sense that *she* is *your* treasure? What do you do to create an environment where she is free to be all that God created her to be? I believe one central way of creating that atmosphere is through prayer. While both spouses should be regularly praying for each other, it is especially important for a man to pray with and for his wife out loud in her presence. This creates intimacy and keeps the relationship honest. Any wife would feel cherished as her husband asks God to give her His graces.

3. She lives faithfully.

The Proverbs 31 woman is not a perfect person. But by grace she has been given a large measure of faithfulness in two areas of life. First, she is a productive provider. It is fair to assume that this is a portrait of productivity covering a lifetime. She isn't doing all of this every day. That would look absurd; what an overwhelming to-do list! This is why ladies have a love-hate relationship with the Proverbs 31 woman. They love what she stands for but hate the fact that they can't come close to pulling it off. But thinking this may cause you to miss the point. The thrust of the passage is that the Proverbs 31 woman embodies wisdom; she is disciplined, diligent.

Second, she is faithful in the details. Old Testament scholar Peter Enns explains that "Proverbs comes at you like life does—lots of seemingly random things, in which it is important to master the details. This lady has mastered the details. To be faithful in the mundane is to be wise. God cares about the details; if God is in your details, He has you. Jesus said, 'if you are faithful in a few things, you'll be faithful in large things.' So you must be careful. Neglect in small things is what comes back to bite you. There may be a small part of life God wants you to master, so it doesn't master you."

Proverbs says charm is deceitful; it promises a lifetime of happiness that it cannot deliver. There is one man who can deliver such a life, Jesus Christ. Let His love fill your heart and you'll be ravishingly beautiful beyond description.

What the Tongue Reveals
Proverbs 18:2,4,6-8,13,20-21,23

If anyone does not stumble in what he says, he is a perfect man, able to bridle the whole body as well. (James 3:1)

A meat thermometer is a great invention. My wife uses one to cook an eye of round to a perfect medium-rare. Its genius is its ability to reveal what is otherwise hidden from your eyes, namely, when the meat is warmed to a delectable tenderness. Is there such a device for the human heart, an instrument that reveals the true nature of what is hidden from our eyes? Yes. The Bible says the tongue reveals the heart. Jesus said, "For the mouth speaks out of that which fills the heart" (Matt. 12:34).

The way you speak reveals what is important to you. Your words betray who or what is ruling your heart, whether people are fundamentally in your way or are there to be blessed by your words, what you think you lack, and who is on the throne of your universe. Most importantly, the tongue reveals your truest religion. There are only two kinds of religions in the world: those based on works or human effort to make one acceptable to God, and the one true religion, which is based on grace, where right standing with God is given as an unearned and undeserved gift through Christ. Listen carefully to the way people speak and you'll know whether they live by grace—they have an acute sense of receiving boundless mercy from the storehouse of God's goodness—or whether they believe they have to prove their worth to God or others.

Do you ever really listen to yourself? What's going on in your heart that you can be:

* Defensive, blame-shifting, or argumentative?

* Self-promoting and demanding, subtly conveying, "Don't challenge or correct me"?

* Complaining, grumbling, fault-finding, or condescending?

* Deftly reminding others how important, or knowledgeable, or gifted, or good you are?

* Gossiping, repeating a bad report about another?

* Always having to give your opinion?

Do you know the reason you're these ways? Your heart is alone, isolated, insecure, needing to prove itself, needing to establish its own worth or value. When we're self-promoting, self-justifying, or self-exalting, it is because the religion ruling our hearts is self-effort, works-based, acceptance before God by performance.

On the contrary, when your heart is warmed by God's grace in Christ, things change. Christians have an experience of being shut up before God. Paul says in Rom. 3:19, "Now we know that whatever the law says, it says to those who are under the law, so that every mouth may be closed and all the world may become accountable to God; because by the works of the law no flesh will be justified in His sight . . . ." The person convicted by God's law, and confident that Christ has fully met the demands of the law in his place and paid the full penalty (death) in his stead for law-breaking, stops talking, as it were, of his own righteousness, and finds a new dynamic at work in the heart—humility, gratitude, and honesty, all expressed in a new way of speaking. This new way of talking

66

reveals one's fundamental sense of who Jesus is. Is He essentially a lawgiver, telling you to do this, stop that, and follow me to perfection? Or is Jesus first and foremost a savior, assuring us that He has perfectly and completely accomplished every requirement for your redemption and set you free? You can usually tell the difference by the way one speaks. (Please don't get me wrong. Of course Jesus is our Lawgiver; He is our Lord. But if your obedience to Him is motivated by proving your worth, you have denied the gospel and turned your obedience into something disdainful before God.)

Proverbs gives you at least four evidences your heart is filled with grace:

1. You know the power of words.

"A fool's mouth is his ruin, and his lips are the snare of his soul" (Prov. 18:7).

"A flattering mouth works ruin" (Prov. 26:28).

"A worthless man digs up evil, while his words are like scorching fire" (Prov. 16:27).

"And the tongue is a fire, the very world of iniquity; the tongue is set among our members as that which defiles the entire body, and sets on fire the course of our life, and is set on fire by hell" (James 3:6).

"The mouth of the righteous is a fountain of life" (Prov. 10:11),

"Death and life are in the power of the tongue" (Prov. 18:21).

These last two verses are most truly fulfilled in Christ. He actually has the ultimate power of death and life in his mouth.

If He gave any of us what we deserved, with one word—guilty!—He could condemn us to death. Instead, Jesus came to earth for sinners with the word of life in His mouth. He spoke to us the word of forgiveness and grace. His promise of grace is the power of eternal life for all who believe the gospel. He is the one true righteous man who gave His life a fountain of eternal life for all who trust in Him.

2. You know the weakness of words.

Words are powerful, but not all-powerful. Proverbs reveals that:

a. Talk is cheap.

"In all labor there is profit, but mere talk leads only to poverty" (Prov. 14:23).

b. Words don't change the facts.

"He who robs his father or his mother and says, 'It is not a transgression,' is the companion of a man who destroys" (Prov. 28:24).

c. Words don't always convey one's true intentions.

"He who conceals hatred has lying lips . . ." (Prov. 10:18).

d. Words can't necessarily force a response from someone.

"A slave will not be instructed by words alone; for though he understands, there will be no response" (Prov. 29:19).

3. You know the marks of speaking wisely.

Wise words are:

a. Honest

"A lying tongue hates those it crushes" (Prov. 26:28).

This verse exposes the motive of lying: hatred. After all, why would we keep the truth from one we love, knowing that the truth sets one free? Also, notice the effect of a lying tongue: it crushes. Just what does lying crush? The verse isn't explicit, but we may surmise that lying crushes trust, the heart of another, one's reputation, one's confidence, and a host of other precious human commodities, depending on the situation.

b. Few

"Where there are many words, transgression is unavoidable, but he who restrains his lips is wise" (Prov. 10:19).

You know how easy it is to get in trouble with your tongue. It is so easy to speak, and so hard to place your words well. It's like golf: it's so easy to hit a ball—it lies right there on the ground and is not moving—but very few people can place it exactly where it's supposed to go.

Where are your words supposed to go? What are your words supposed to do? You shouldn't use them until you know, right? The point is, if you talk too quickly, you may not know.

"He who restrains his words has knowledge, and he who has a cool spirit is a man of understanding" (Prov. 17:27).

God wants your words to be primarily for healing:

"A soothing (healing) tongue is a tree of life" (Prov. 15:4).

Most of us err in one of two directions: we say too little or we say too much. I've yet to see a Bible verse condemning those who say too little. Almost comically, "less is more" according to Prov. 17:28: "Even a fool, when he is silent, is considered wise; when he closes his lips he is considered prudent." But, Prov. 29:20 bluntly warns: "Do you see a man who is hasty in his words? There is more hope for a fool than for him."

"A fool does not delight in understanding, but only in revealing his own mind" (Prov. 18:2). This verse, a sure marker of self-centeredness, condemns you if you feel called to give a running commentary on everything going on around you, or if you believe your opinion is so important that everyone needs to hear it all the time. What would happen if you gave your opinion only when you were asked? If you're quick to say what you want whenever you want, you've entered the danger zone: "Death and life are in the power of the tongue, and those who love it will eat its fruit" (Prov. 18:21). Your most plentiful resource, words, is also your most potent. One of the traits that sets you apart in creation as exceedingly glorious, the power to speak and to edify others, also makes you most lethal.

c. Calm

"A gentle answer turns away wrath, but a harsh word stirs up anger" (Prov. 15:1).

I have to drive through a residential neighborhood every week to pick up the church bulletin from the printer's home. I confess that I normally zip in and zip out from the main road. Translated, I roll through the stop signs and exceed the speed limit. One day I noticed a man waiting in his car on the street as I left the house where I get the bulletins. I thought perhaps he needed directions. I approached his car and he asked me whether I lived in the neighborhood. I explained that I did not. He said, not in the happiest tone, "I know. You speed in and out of here every week, disregarding the stop signs and the neighbors, and you create a safety hazard for our children." I'd say he was ready for a fight. But even though my pride welled up within me in momentary denial, I couldn't argue with him; he was absolutely right. I said, "You're right, I'm sorry. I have been disrespectful to this neighborhood, and it is flat-out wrong. Please forgive me." I really doubt he was expecting that response. Immediately he backed off and toned down. Yet I persisted to maintain my guilt and apologized again, and thanked him for warning me before anything serious happened. He dropped it and went on his way. The only way to account for my "abnormal" behavior is the grace of God and the Holy Spirit bringing this verse to mind as soon as the man confronted me.

d. Appropriate

"A man has joy in an apt answer, and how delightful is a timely word!" (Prov. 15:23).

"Like apples of gold in settings of silver is a word spoken in right circumstances" (Prov. 25:11).

e. Measured

"The heart of the righteous ponders how to answer, but the mouth of the wicked pours out evil things" (Prov. 15:28).

"The heart of the wise instructs his mouth and adds persuasiveness to his lips" (Prov. 16:23).

This tends to fly in the face of our culture's esteem of quick wit and instant responses or put-downs, especially as seen on sitcoms.

f. Effective

"Sweetness of speech increases persuasiveness" (Prov. 16:21).

"The tongue of the wise makes knowledge acceptable" (Prov. 15:2).

"A soft tongue breaks the bone (of another's stubbornness)" (Prov. 25:15).

4. You know the glory of edifying words.

When we are motivated to put down others with our words, to answer tit-for-tat, we feel a temporary sense of pleasure or victory. But what have we truly accomplished? What glory is there in seemingly putting another in his or her place? Does that make us better people? Are we smarter or more moral for having done so? Whose job is that, anyway? When we aim to hurt with our words, when we are guilty of "arguing ad hominem" (proving a point by attacking the person), we've only shown our hearts to be as petty as the person we feel the need to malign. Paul instructs us "to malign no one, to be peaceable, gentle, showing every consideration for all men" (Titus 3:2). God is very jealous for our words to reveal the power and beauty of His words, and the Word made flesh, Jesus Christ:

"The tongue of the wise brings healing" (Prov. 12:18).

"Pleasant words are a honeycomb" (Prov. 16:24).

"The lips of the righteous feed many" (Prov. 10:21).

"The teaching of the wise is a fountain of life" (Prov. 13:14).

"Anxiety in a man's heart weighs it down, but a good word makes it glad" (Prov. 12:25).

"There is gold, and an abundance of jewels, but the lips of knowledge are a more precious thing" (Prov. 20:15).

Each of these verses depicts the speaking ministry of Jesus.

Do your homework and think soberly about the way you speak to others. Are your words devouring others' needs or meeting them? "There is a kind of man whose teeth are like swords, and his jaw teeth like knives, to devour the afflicted from the earth and the needy from among men" (Prov. 30:14).

Are you careful to consider what various situations demand? "Like apples of gold in settings of silver is a word spoken in right circumstances" (Prov. 25:11). How often is what you say the right word? When do you really need criticism, gossip, complaining, grumbling, labeling others, giving your opinion when unsolicited? No wonder Proverbs 21:23 says: "He who guards his mouth and his tongue guards his soul from troubles." Watch what you say, and look into your heart for the motives for your words.

When we're honest with ourselves, we must admit we're careless with our words. We need to be saved from the guilt of our speaking. No one lives like we've just described . . . no one except Jesus. The Word made flesh, the Eternal Logos, came speaking to us the word of healing, the word for the right circumstance, the word we desperately needed, the word for salvation, the golden apple of the gospel. As Peter confessed, "Lord, to whom shall we go? You have words of eternal life" (John 6:68). Peter knew that Jesus never wasted, misplaced, or misspoke a single word in order that He might save us from our sins. When Jesus is yours through faith, He'll guard your soul where you can't. You'll know He's there by your quickness—quick to listen, quick to speak less, quick to use words as an instrument employed every day for His glory and for the edification of others, to give them grace, according to the need of the moment (Eph. 4:29).

The Dangers of Money

The rich man is wise in his own eyes,
but the poor who has understanding sees through him.
(Proverbs 28:11)

A few years ago, my son Luke entered a photography contest in a magazine. The issue revealing the winners finally arrived. He wasn't one of them, but he should have been. In my judgment, several of his pictures were better than any of the winners. Do you think I can be objective about that? Of course not. Luke is my son. Naturally I believe his pictures are better. No doubt there are other things in life about which I could be more objective. In the grand scheme of things, it isn't a big deal that I'm biased about my son's pictures. However, it is a big deal to be objective about issues along the path of life that easily cause us to stumble. Therefore, the more important the issue, the greater the need for objectivity.

Objective about Wealth?

Can you and I be objective, for example, about wealth--its benefits and hazards? That's an important question. If any of us has any measure of wealth, or aspirations to be well-off, we need to be objective about the power, nature, and effect of wealth on our motives and perspectives. What does the Bible say? Can any of us assess the hazards and benefits of wealth objectively? Are we innately able to negotiate the waters of wealth in the wisest fashion? The Bible says no. The problem is with our hearts. Our hearts are easily deceived about what's best for us; the wise person knows this. "Every man's way is right in his own eyes" (Prov. 21:2).

So what should we do? Lay hold of a promise: "Those who seek the Lord understand all things" (Prov. 28:5). When we understand wealth from God's perspective, when we measure wealth in the course of our seeking the Lord, and only then, we will see clearly enough its true benefits and hazards. Notice how Lady Wisdom is presented to us: "She is more precious than jewels; and nothing you desire compares with her. Long life is in her right hand; in her left hand are riches and honor . . . . happy are all who hold her fast" (Prov. 3:15-16, 18). To understand wealth, you first need to make a comparison between Wisdom and wealth. Which do you really believe is more desirable? Do you honestly think no amount of wealth, however you measure it, can compare to the surpassing, incomparable value of the Lord God, Wisdom incarnate?

This verse also makes an explicit promise: if you take wealth from Wisdom's hand, you'll be happy (which is, naturally, what you're desiring). It also gives an implicit warning: if you take wealth from your own hand, you're in trouble (which is, naturally, what you want to avoid).

The key question, therefore, is, How do you know when you understand wealth objectively? What is the evidence you are taking your wealth from God's hand, on His terms, according to His dictates, and not your own? Money taken out of God's hand is safe; money taken from your own is dangerous. Many of the verses in Proverbs about money constitute tests to help you determine this. Consider these four:

1. Do you resist the fact that this chapter is about money—or are you truly appreciative for your own safety?

"The rich man is wise in his own eyes" (Prov. 28:11).

Have you confessed the sin of greed to anyone? Do you feel protective of your money and autonomous over its use, or do you routinely submit significant expenditures to God? You are on unstable footing if your fundamental attitude is, No one has the right to tell me what to do with my money.

2. Are you in a hurry to obtain wealth?

"A faithful man will abound with blessings, but he who makes haste to be rich will not go unpunished. . . . A man with an evil eye hastens after wealth and does not know that want will come upon him" (Prov. 28:20, 22).

Are you patient with your station in life, or in debt up to your eyeballs trying to live beyond the lifestyle God has allotted to you? We live in a culture that encourages us to have everything now. Just put those purchases on a credit card and worry about it later. The pain and suffering resulting from such folly is incalculable, not to mention the magnitude of the slavery that ensues: "The rich rules over the poor, and the borrower becomes the lender's slave" (Prov. 22:7).

3. Is sorrow in your wealth?

"It is the blessing of the Lord which makes rich, and He adds no sorrow to it" (Prov. 10:22).

What sort of sorrow is the sage envisioning? Perhaps sorrow because you don't have more? Sorry that you might lose some of it? Sorrow relationally because you love money more than people? Sorrow experienced because you acquired what you thought would make you happy (a new car, house, vacation, jewelry, etc.) and you felt empty soon afterward? The point remains clear. God is the source of wealth, He gives it because He delights to, and He doesn't give it to make us sorrowful. If your wealth is accompanied by sorrow it is a likely indicator you have received it (ungratefully) or use it (selfishly, unwisely, impulsively) in a way contrary to God's plan.

4. Do you know the power of money?

Have you ever seen a parent give his little child a chainsaw to play with? It will be a tragic day when a parent puts a 16" chainsaw in a toddler's hands, starts it, and says, "Have fun! Go for it!" Why? Because it would be so utterly foolish. A chainsaw is an extremely dangerous tool even for a person who knows how to use it, let alone a child who would instinctively make it a toy. You don't need a PhD to see the principle involved here: never put a dangerous, powerful tool in the hands of someone incapable of safely handling it. The stronger the force, the greater the power to tempt us and to pull us off the safe way to live. Money, like a chainsaw, can be a powerful tool for blessing or a lethal weapon to harm. Remembering that sin's nature is to deceive, we need to ask the question, How does sin deceive us concerning money?

The Deception of Money Misused

Let's explore four truths presented in Proverbs concerning the power of money:

1. The heart's tendency is to make money a false security.

"He who trusts in his riches will fall, but the righteous will flourish like the green leaf" (Prov. 11:28).

Why should you be concerned about trusting riches? Because it is so easy to do. The heart incessantly longs to trust something. Sin loves to trust the tangible--something I can see, feel, handle, or smell. Money gives me freedom, power, and choices; it allows me to plan for tomorrow and to enjoy today (not necessarily bad in itself). Money creates independence, something we all crave, and therefore is extremely hard to give up. I remember the first time I went crabbing as a child. We tied fish heads to strings, threw them into the water, waited for the tug, and then gently pulled in the string. To my surprise, the crab wouldn't let go! He dug his bluish claws into that fish head like it was the last morsel in the bay and looked up at me as if to say, "It's mine, how dare you!" What he thought was a meal actually became a prison. Jesus met a rich man just like that. " 'Sell all that you possess and distribute it to the poor, and you shall have treasure in heaven; and come, follow Me' " (Luke 18:22). He couldn't do it. He was slave to his wealth; he didn't own it, it owned him!

Is wealth the problem here? It may be tempting to think so, but that would miss the truth. Both rich and poor, and everyone in between can be tempted by money. Our hearts are the problem; we are so deceitful that we abuse all sorts of things to our detriment. If money itself was the problem the Bible would exhort us to strive for poverty (which it does not do) and would not make statements such as:

"It is the blessing of the Lord that makes rich" (Prov. 10:22).

"The generous man will be prosperous" (Prov. 11:25).

"Great wealth is in the house of the righteous" (Prov. 15:6).

"A good man leaves an inheritance to his children's children" (Prov. 13:22).

It is one thing to enjoy humbly the blessing, quite another to make it a security. We know it is becoming a security when money is making us single-minded: "I'll get it at all costs; I'll protect it at all costs." Therefore, God warns: "Do not weary yourself to gain wealth, cease from your consideration of it" (Prov. 23:4). Only a self-deceived heart would refuse to believe the sober warnings of the Bible: "Make sure that your character is free from the love of money" (Heb. 13:5). "But those who want to get rich fall into temptation and a snare and many foolish and harmful desires which plunge men into ruin and destruction. For the love of money is a root of all sorts of evil . . . ." (1 Tim. 6:9-10).

Money is a false security in two other ways. First, it is possible we could lose it somehow. Through lawsuits, medical costs, financial crises, theft, etc., people lose money. I pastored a brilliant engineer who, just on the eve of retirement, lost all of it to the Enron scandal. Second, money doesn't deliver what it promises. One wealthy man was asked, "How much money is enough?" He answered, "Just a little bit more," which comports with Proverbs 23:5: "When you set your eyes on it [wealth], it is gone. For wealth certainly makes itself wings, like an eagle that flies toward the heavens." How different your spending attitudes would be if you fully embraced this truth: "For we have brought nothing into the world, so we cannot take anything out of it either" (1 Tim.6:7).

2. The heart uses wealth to escape reality.

"A rich man's wealth is his strong city, and like a high wall in his own imagination" (Prov. 18:11).

Wealth has the power to create in us a sense that we are far better off than we actually are: preaching to the mind, as it were, an impregnable strength. It creates a false standard of measuring one's worth before God: "I'm so materially well-off, I must also be spiritually well-off with God." Perhaps this accounts for why so few wealthy people feel the need for God. Jesus explicitly told the rich young ruler: " 'How hard it is for those who are wealthy to enter the kingdom of God' " (Luke 18:24). In fact, most Americans are relatively in the same position. When was the last time you sincerely asked God for your "daily bread"? Proverbs warns for a good reason:

80

"Riches do not profit in the day of wrath" (Prov. 11:4).

We can't let outward religious practice fool us, either. In Luke 16 we're told that the Pharisees loved money. Verse 15 defines the heart of the Pharisee religion: "You are those who justify yourselves in the sight of men." Do you think there is a connection between their feeling secure morally in God's sight, and their lust for money? Any reality is a false reality until our creaturely dependence upon the Lord is at the heart of it. You'll know what strikes at the heart of a person's reality by the way he talks about wealth and God. Richard Baxter, an English Puritan centuries ago, wrote:

> *In their entertainments, visitations and converse, how rare is serious, holy conference among them! How seldom do you hear them remembering their guests and companions of the presence of the holy God; of the necessity of renewing, confirming and assisting grace; of the riches of Christ revealed in the gospel; of the endless life of joy or misery which is at hand! How seldom do you hear them seriously assisting each other in the examination of their hearts, and making their calling and election sure, and preparing for the day of death and judgment! A word or two in private with some zealous minister or friend, is almost all the pious conference that shall be heard from some of the better sort of them. . . . The honest, heart-warming, heavenly discourse that is usual among poor serious Christians, would seem, at the tables of most of our great ones, but an unseasonable interruption of their more natural and acceptable kind of converse.*

(quoted in Tim Keller's <u>Ministries of Mercy</u>)

3. The heart believes wealth sets one above the law.

"The rich man is wise in his own eyes, but the poor man

who has understanding sees through him" (Prov. 28:11),

There lies a thought within all of us, "Don't tell me how to use my money!" It is an extension of our propensity to autonomy: "I'll run my life the way I want to!" When "my money" is a lot of money, the idea becomes larger than reality. You may have heard about diplomatic immunity. In the Washington, D.C., area, foreign diplomats are immune from all traffic laws and tickets. Guess what? They park and drive however they want! That illustrates how power corrupts. What motivates "white collar" crime? Isn't it normally people in power positions who think they are above the rules? Wealth has a way of eating at the integrity of the heart; it sticks its claws on a person's integrity and tries to squeeze out a compromise with principle. "Better is the poor who walks in his integrity, than he who is crooked, though he be rich" (Prov. 28:6).

4. The heart deceived by wealth is isolated from the heart of God.

One of the clearest revelations of God's heart in the Bible is its closeness to the poor. Tragically, one of the clearest revelations of the heart of the rich is their indifference to the poor.

"He who gives to the poor will never want, but he who shuts his eyes will have many curses" (Prov. 28:27).

"He who oppresses the poor taunts his Maker, but he who is gracious to the needy honors Him" (Prov. 14:31).

"One who is gracious to a poor man lends to the Lord, and He will repay him for his deed" (Prov. 19:17).

One wise man knew that money, much or little, created a temptation to deceive him:

"Two things I asked of You, do not refuse me before I die: keep deception and lies far from me, give me neither poverty nor riches; feed me with the food that is my portion, that I not be full and deny You and say, 'Who is the Lord?' or that I not be in want and steal, and profane the name of my God" (Prov. 30:7-9). Can you earnestly pray this contentment prayer? We all want to believe we're the exception: try me, Lord, I can handle wealth. How many people do you know who have significantly scaled back their lifestyles after amassing substantial wealth?

What kind of person prays this way?

It is not natural to us to pray like this. It is much more our tendency to want blessings, and lots of them. The Christian message that is laced with wealth and prosperity is very popular, even though Jesus never asked anyone to follow him and then promised wealth, but rather called people to die.

Here are several characteristics of the kind of person who prays this way:

They are wise. This prayer comes up in the wisdom literature of the bible. The person who is bold enough to pray this buys the notion of biblical wisdom. Without the inventor's manual we are going to get it wrong. God made the world and to enjoy it most fully we do so on his terms. The fool says, it doesn't matter if I didn't make the world, I can figure this out on my own. The fool will have no one tell him how to find happiness.

They know themselves well. They are skeptical of their own motives because they know how deceitful the heart can be. They know there is no reason for them to be exempt from humanity's proclivity to underestimate the power of money. Notice the tone of desperation here: "*don't refuse me*"! This healthy skepticism frees him to be honest, transparent; did you notice, he is talking about money. Most of us would rather not.

They believe in God's power and purposes. That's why they pray; they know God can do anything, and that he responds to the requests of his people to fulfill his good purposes for them.

Because God is true and trustworthy, they rely on his word as that infallible interpreter of all things necessary for life and godliness. So Prov. 30:5-6: "Every word of God is tested; he is a shield to those who take refuge in Him. Do not add to His words lest he reprove you, and you be proved a liar."

They have a measured sense of life's span. Agur says, "*don't refuse me before I die.*" His perspective seems to be, what I am asking for is necessary for all my life, not just when I am young or old. Whether you are young and ambitious and trying to achieve the standard of living of your parents, or when you are empty nesters with a greater amount of disposal income, wealth is a temptation.

What are the requests?

There are two, *keep* and *give*. Each gets a little elaboration. *Keep* deals with the heart, especially motives. *Give* deals with circumstances. What connects them to each other? It is our attitude or expectation that governs how we respond in specific circumstances. Your character determines how you respond in circumstances.

Keep deception and lies far from me.
Deception and lies are two related words forming one idea, according to Waltke, deceit that takes the form of a verbal lie. Why pray this? Because certain ideas seem valid, but upon close inspection prove to be lies. Some ideas are very appealing to us, and can fool us into being true, when they are not. So he prays, keep them far from me.

How would you recognize a lie about money from a truth? Only by what God's word says about it—and everything God says about it, not just select things. We could go to passages which may easily lead you to think God wants you rich, while other passages lead you to think he wants you poor. The main point is this: if you have no intimate, working relationship with God's word, you will likely be deceived by money. But, just

84

because you know God's word doesn't guarantee his truth controls your heart.

What lies tempt you and me?

> If I'm poor I won't worry about money.
> God wants me rich.
> I'll be happy and content with more money.
> The more I get the more I'll give.

These are so seductive we need God's word as the only infallible source of understanding. Lies live best among the self-deceived. Hence the warning of Prov. 30:12, "There is a kind who is pure in his own eyes, yet is not washed from his filthiness," echoing Prov. 14:12, "There is a way which seems right to a man, but in the end it is the way of death." Do you believe you are fundamentally prone to underestimate the power of money over you? If not, you don't know your self well. The wise person says, yes, keep me from lies. They are too strong for me, I am too weak for them.

Give me neither poverty nor riches, feed me with the food that is my portion.
Give means to provide anew with; to cause to receive. This sounds like Jesus' prayer in Matt.6:11: "give us this day our daily bread." We can ask God for what we need, for our portion. Food is probably a literary device called synecdoche, part for the whole. Food is one part of the whole, all of our needs. God is committed to meeting the essential needs of his creatures- food, shelter, clothing. He gives food to all of us, beast and human alike. He feeds the ravens and clothes the lilies. Therefore Paul can exhort us, "If we have food and shelter, with these we shall be content." (1 Tim.6:8)

Agur's prayer looks like a plea for contentment: desiring what you have, not desiring what you don't have. Then he gives his reasons why contentment is a safe place for his heart. He lists two extremes, poverty and wealth.

Poverty may drive him to steal to meet his needs. It deceives us by justifying desperate measures to meet essential needs. That would be tantamount to profaning God's name, that is, saying something about him that is not true. If you say you believe in God, yet steal, you're saying either God is not good and won't provide your basic needs, or that God's law is trivial and ought to be broken, since stealing is forbidden in the Ten Commandments.

To be satisfied, on the other hand, or *full,* tends toward neglecting the provider. To say *who is the Lord* is to forget where the blessings come from. Who is he? Never forget to answer! He is my provider, the determiner of my gifts, income, and welfare. It is to be deceived into thinking you are in control or self-sufficient. When we are full we tend toward complacency. Urgency is lost. A stomach at ease portends to a heart at ease.

What ought you to say when you are full?
 Thank you, I am tremendously blessed to have this.
 Why me? I don't deserve this!
 Let me give back to you in proportion to how full I am.

Moses warned Israel about this in Dt. 8:17-18:
"You may say in your heart, 'My power and the strength of my hand made me this wealth.' But you shall remember the Lord your God, for it is He who is giving you power to make wealth, that he may confirm his covenant which He swore to your fathers…"

Here is an irony. God does indeed give the blessings, but they are inherently powerful. It is the same with wealth as it is with time, sex, food, words, and many other things.

To be full is a metaphor for wealth. How does wealth deceive? Wealth is like medicine. Before you use it, you need to know the side effects. Side effects are the manifestations you can expect, the ways your being will be influenced, by the benefit you receive from the medicine. Wealth has benefits. But they are only truly enjoyed when you are cautious about the side effects.

Agur's contentment is motivated by the glory of God. That is his greatest concern, an authentic expression of faith. He knows only God can save him from the power of human greed. You could call this humble ambition:

Work hard? Yes!

Save money? Yes!

Have enough for your grandchildren? Yes!

Ever vigilant over wealth's deceptive power? Yes!

If you've given me wealth, Lord, it is for your glory. Now let me live and give to your glory.

How Do You Know Money Is Deceiving Your Heart?

Here are two tests to help you determine whether money is deceiving you:

1. Examine what you are willing to trade for it.

It is amazing how some people confuse the value of money with other things. Have you read stories about parents selling their children? How many times do people trade their integrity for money? How many families are fractured by bitterness over the settling of an estate? How many children have been emotionally orphaned because their father sacrificed his family on the altar of work? Is that lost perspective? Consider that one financial tycoon was quoted as saying, "No one on their deathbed says, 'I wish I'd spent more time at the office.'" People will kill, lie, cheat, slander, and risk their reputation for money. What power! They will even rob God:

"Will a man rob God? Yet you are robbing Me! But you say, 'How have we robbed You?' In tithes and offerings" (Mal. 3:8).

Proverbs presents simple options that expose our ultimate values:

Would you rather be wealthy than wise?

"Take my instruction and not silver, and knowledge rather than choicest gold. For wisdom is better than jewels; and all desirable things can not compare with her" (Prov. 8:10-11).

Are you willing to compromise honesty for money?

"Better is the poor who walks in his integrity than he who is crooked though he be rich" (Prov. 28:6).

Would you sacrifice the fear of the Lord?

"Better is a little with the fear of the Lord than great treasure and turmoil with it" (Prov. 15:16).

Would you ditch justice to increase your net worth?

"Better is a little with righteousness than great income with injustice" (Prov. 16:8).

2. Examine your generosity.

There is only one way to know whether your money owns you: scrutinize your willingness to part with it. If you can't be generous, you are its slave. Be careful here. Some people measure generosity by what they give away. The Bible doesn't do accounting that way. Generosity is marked not by how much you give away, but by what you give up. If your giving costs you nothing, it isn't generosity. King David needed to make an offering to the Lord and Araunah tried to give him the necessary animals as a gift (2 Sam. 24:24). David would have none of it: "No, but I will surely buy it from you for a price, for I will not offer burnt offerings to the Lord my God which cost me nothing."

In Luke 21 Jesus tells the story of the widow's mite. Who gave generously to God, the poor lady with a few cents or the rich people with their thousands of dollars? Generosity is not measured by how much one gives, but by how much one gives up. "[The rich] all out of their surplus put into the offering; but she out of her poverty put in all that she had to live on" (Luke 21:4). Paul found such faith among the Macedonian believers "that in a great ordeal of affliction their abundance of joy and their deep poverty overflowed in the wealth of their liberality. For I testify that according to their ability, and beyond their ability, they gave of their own accord, begging us with much urging for the favor of participation in the support of the saints" (2 Cor. 8:2-4).

When I interview folks for membership in my church I always ask them about their giving practices. Not how much they give--I don't need or want to know that--but what they believe in principle God wants them to give. This is justified, I believe, by one of the five membership vows in my denomination, which reads, "Do you promise to support the worship and work of the church to the best of your ability?" It doesn't make sense to have folks commit to the ministry of the church who have no intention of taking seriously their stewardship. Once I interviewed a young couple with three children plus a newborn. The man was in law school. Their monthly income was $40. Yes, that is not a typo, it was $40. To my utter amazement they told me they tithed on that money.

The Glory of Money Well-used

1. Our use of money is a window for the world to see God.

Any parent whose child excels in something (sports, music, art, drama, science, etc.) eventually experiences the familiar "that's my boy" sort of pride. They're proud because their children reveal to the watching world something good about them--why else be proud? In the same way, a Christian's use of money tells the watching world what God is like. We who have the privilege of using concrete resources for God's kingdom either honor or dishonor Him by our giving: "Honor the Lord from your wealth and from the first of all your produce . . . " (Prov. 3:9).

Our giving says a lot about God. When we are generous and faithful with our resources we reveal that God is the owner of all things and a wonderful provider. But how does anyone know what I give? They may not know what you give, but they probably have a good idea what you spend some of your money to buy. This verse, in its historical context, was given to an agrarian society. The tithe was fruit, vegetables, and wine brought into the storehouse for the priests and the poor. What Joe Israelite brought in was no secret; nor was it hidden whether he brought the firstfruits, the best of the crops. The point is, unbelieving neighbors are watching and they may be wondering: what kind of God do they worship? Do we look like all the other materialists in our culture? What does your lifestyle say about your faith, ultimate trust, priorities, and belief about what God has done for you? Has He withheld His best and firstfruits from you?

2. Well-used money builds faith.

The point of the firstfruits is faith. When you give away the first portion of the harvest, you're trusting that the rest will be available for your needs when it's time. God will have to preserve the rest of the harvest. Does He love you enough to do that? Is He powerful enough to do that? God is Jehovah-Jireh, Yahweh our provider, who knows how to make things stretch (if need be) to the end of the month. Faith is forged not when we write checks out of our abundance, but in the furnace of need and provision. I have had the enormous privilege as a pastor to watch young couples struggle financially, yet remain faithful to give generously to the church. While in a few extreme cases our mercy fund has helped some in crisis, I have never seen one of them become destitute. You cannot out-give God! Do you know that experientially, or as simply a mental abstraction?

In the spirit of Malachi 3:10 (" 'Bring the whole tithe into the storehouse, so that there may be food in My house, and test Me now in this,' says the Lord of hosts, 'if I will not open for you the windows of heaven, and pour out for you a blessing until it overflows.' "), I urge you to test God in this. Start with the basics. Make the first check you write after payday, if you don't already, your tithe check. Then have something set aside for spontaneous opportunities to give, and pray for God to bring them providentially to you and for wisdom to recognize them.

Here is one example from my life. After officiating at a funeral I was given an unusually large honorarium. I'm certain that was largely because of the distance I had to travel to the service. The amount was $400. My first inclination was to get some nicer golf clubs. I didn't need that money to meet my daily needs. Yet immediately the Lord challenged me to give it all away. I did, discreetly, within a week, having heard of a need in the church. Within the next month or so I officiated at two other funerals, and again received what I would consider to be unusually generous honorariums. Because a pastor's work includes "marrying and burying," one really expects nothing. But in each case I was given $200, thus "replacing" the $400 given away a month earlier. Although sometimes I'm really thick about noticing these kinds of things, this time I saw the connection. The Lord prompted me to give the first $400, then gave it right back to me. So it was clear to me that I should give away the next $400 too, which I did.

Then a month or so passed. My wife's car broke down on her way to school. Mercifully, it died only 100 yards from a repair shop I had used before we moved from that area of town. I asked whether they could get it to their shop and work on it, and they assured me they could. By the end of the day the problem was diagnosed. The fuel pump had failed. The shop owner, however, noticed that the car was only about a thousand miles beyond its warranty, so he called a friend at a Chevy dealership (not the one where I purchased the car). The dealer agreed to fix it for free, treating it as if our car was still under warranty. The dealer didn't have to, mind you. The reason, apparently, was the relationship the shop owner had with the dealer. If the car had broken down any other place, who knows whether the dealer would have been called?

What's the point of the story? You can never out-give God. Guess how much the repair job would have cost me? I saw the invoice, which was for $800, the amount God in His grace led me to give away before all this happened!

3. Money well-used reveals the work of Christ.

When the day is over we must confess that we are dull of heart and slow to trust. We tend to love our wealth (Americans are wealthy compared with the rest of the world) and trust in it. I've not met many Christians who appeared to give away their money in proportion to the sacrifice of their Savior. Salvation is about sacrifice. So is biblical giving. We've not given our hearts to God as He deserves, and we're guilty. The glory of the gospel is that Jesus stepped in where we deserved to go. He set aside the riches of His glory in heaven to come to earth to live a life of economic poverty. No one could accuse Jesus of misusing wealth. His entire ministry, He depended on the gifts of others. He had nowhere to lay His head. He knew material poverty, but this is not what counts. He willingly knew spiritual poverty, taking upon Himself the wrath our sins deserved:

"For you know the grace of our Lord Jesus Christ, that though He was rich, yet for your sakes He became poor, so that you through His poverty might become rich" (2 Cor. 8:9).

Jesus could have asked the Father, How much should I give? The question was never up for discussion. He came to give it all away, for only by His perfect obedience and sinless death on the cross could He atone for the greed and guilt of sinners like us.

You should ask the Lord what you should give. If you feel the pull of your money resisting the question, you may need to ask Jesus for a new heart. Robert Murray M'Cheyne wrote:

> "I fear there are many hearing me who may know well that they are not Christians, because they do not love to give. To give largely and liberally, not grudgingly at all, requires a new heart; an old heart would rather part with its life-blood than its money. Oh my friends! enjoy your money; make the most of it; give none away; enjoy it quickly for I can tell you, you will be beggars throughout eternity." (quoted in Tim Keller's *Ministries of Mercy*)

Your money is a chainsaw; used wisely, it will cut paths of joy and righteousness. Used carelessly, it will certainly hurt you. Wisdom teaches us those distinctions. Wisdom says, First give yourself to the Lord, saturate your wealth with Christ's riches for you, and you'll know how to give.

Case Study: A Rich Fool's Wealth

But God said to him, "You fool! This very night your soul is required of you; and now who will own what you have prepared?"
So is the man who stores up treasure for himself, and is not rich toward God. (Luke 12:20-21)

Because both my father and my oldest brother were trained in law, I've heard many times the saying: the man who represents himself in a court of law has a fool for a client. Why would you talk *only to yourself* about your legal case? That does seem foolish.

Why would you talk *only to yourself* about your money? Jesus says that, too, is foolish. It springs off the page in this parable. The man is reasoning to himself, consulting himself; he is his own attorney, judge and jury. Therefore, naturally, he always gets the verdict he desires.

Who should you be talking to about your money?

The answer to that question actually starts in verse 13. "Teacher, tell my brother to divide the family inheritance with me." Jesus is speaking to a crowd about very important matters of the soul, and a man interrupts him with a question about . . . money! Apparently his older brother wants to keep the family estate together (the honorable course of action), but he demands his share of the inheritance, which probably would have been land. The impropriety of the interruption is like the doctor explaining how to give critical, life-saving medicine to your child, but you interrupt him to ask him who he thinks is going to win the Super Bowl.

Jesus rebuffs him (v. 14), essentially saying, I didn't come for that; I came to reconcile people to each other. It is true, rabbis gave legal rulings on such matters. But Jesus has something better for the man, something far better than any amount of inheritance: a warning about greed. "Be on your guard against every form of greed" (Luke 12:15).

Jesus is saying, You're worried about your father's inheritance--it's consuming you, it owns you--you need to be more concerned that your greed for that inheritance will disinherit you from the kingdom of God.

Although the presenting issue in this encounter is money, it's not the root problem. The real issue is, You're not thinking wisely about your soul, and inheriting the kingdom of heaven. What's the proof of that? "Not even when one has an abundance does his life consist of his possessions" (Luke 12:15). Yes, everyone needs a minimum amount to live, but more goods never translate to abundant life.

Your problems are not solved even if you get the inheritance. Your desire for things will prove insatiable. A wealthy man was asked, How much money is enough? He answered, Just a little more!

Your dreams of the abundant life won't be fulfilled with abundance.

Do you see the issue? Of what does your life, your soul, consist?

You need to know this so you can know what is preserving your soul or what is destroying your soul. See the comparison: "for not even when one has an abundance does his life consist of his posessions"; therefore, greed for possessions can destroy it. So Jesus warns, "Be on your guard against every form of greed" (Luke 12:15). Greed is lusting for what God hasn't given you, or discontent with what God has given you. Greed will destroy you, in any of its forms, and there must be many: greed that tempts the poor, the rich, and everyone between. Do you know what form of greed tempts you? Do you know any person who has and wants less? Invariably, the more we get the more we want. Do you know any people who have self-consciously refused to increase their standard of living, despite gaining increased income, so they can invest more in the kingdom of God?

Jesus tells a parable to illustrate greed.

And He told them a parable, saying, 'The land of a rich man was very productive. And he began reasoning to himself, saying, 'What shall I do, since I have no place to store my crops?' Then he said, 'I will tear down my barns and build larger ones, and there I will store all my grain and my goods.' " (Luke 12:16-17)

Notice that the man reasons to himself, he talks to his soul. I'm sure that comes naturally; we're born as our own infallible interpreters of reality.

"All the ways of a man are clean in his own sight . . . " (Prov. 16:2).

"The rich man is wise in his own eyes . . ." (Prov. 28:11).

Remember that I said he is talking to the wrong person? With whom should he be reasoning? Do you talk to your stock broker about your health? Do you consult your doctor about your car? Do you think he should consult the person ultimately responsible for creating the wealth? "It is the blessing of the Lord that makes rich" (Prov. 10:22).

Shouldn't he being talking to God?

97

Significantly, the subject of the first sentence in the parable is the land. "The land of a rich man was very productive." Whose land is it, ultimately?

"The earth is the Lord's, and all it contains" (Ps. 24:1).

At the end of the day, there is one reason why he had a bumper crop: God made the earth fertile, God made seeds to sprout, God sent the rain, God caused the sun to shine, God moderated the temperature, God gave him the means to harvest it, and God endowed him with the intelligence to think carefully about farming. God deserves all the glory.

> *He causes the grass to grow for the cattle, and vegetation for the labor of man, so that he may bring forth food from the earth. (Ps. 104:14)*

> *He changes a wilderness into a pool of water and a dry land into springs of water; and there He makes the hungry to dwell, so that they may establish an inhabited city, and sow fields and plant vineyards, and gather a fruitful harvest. Also He blesses them and they multiply greatly, and He does not let their cattle decrease. (Ps. 107:35-38)*

> *And yet He did not leave himself without witness, in that He did good and gave you rains from heaven and fruitful seasons, satisfying your hearts with food and gladness. (Acts 14:17)*

The wise person delights in these truths, moves in concert with them, and governs his passions accordingly.

What should he have said?

God, thank you, you gave me this bumper crop. Bumper

crops are good, wonderful gifts from your hand. What do you want me to do with all of this? I am merely a steward of the riches entrusted to me.

King David knew how to answer that question:

Yours, O LORD, is the greatness and the power and the glory and the victory and the majesty, indeed everything that is in the heavens and the earth; Yours is the dominion, O LORD, and You exalt Yourself as head over all. Both riches and honor come from You, and You rule over all, and in Your hand is power and might; and it lies in Your hand to make great and to strengthen everyone. Now therefore, our God, we thank You, and praise Your glorious name. But who am I and who are my people that we should be able to offer as generously as this? For all things come from You, and from Your hand we have given You. (1 Chron. 29:11-14)

Did you ever realize that when you place money in the offering plate, although you physically take it out of your wallet, in an ultimate sense you took it out of God's hand and put it back into His hand?

What would God say in response?

That depends on what God really cares about. The Bible says He cares about the welfare of that man, the welfare of his fellow man, and welfare of the entire culture. Hence the warning in Proverbs 11:25-26:

The generous man will be prosperous, and he who waters will himself be watered. He who withholds grain, the people will curse him, but blessing will be on the head of him who sells it.

Based on the testimony of Scripture, it is reasonable to assume God would warn him:

> *From everyone who has been given much, much will be required . . . .* (Luke 12:48)

> *He who loves money will not be satisfied with money, nor he who loves abundance with its income.* (Eccl. 5:10)

> *The love of money is a root of all sorts of evil.* (1 Tim. 6:10)

> *Make sure your character is free from the love of money, being content with what you have . . . .* (Heb. 13:5)

God certainly says to us, I've been generous to you, so you be generous to others. "Honor the Lord from your wealth and from the first of all your produce . . ." (Prov. 3:9). So give it away, help people start their own businesses, build a gym for the local church, or fund the planting of churches all over the world.

Why wouldn't you talk to God about your wealth? Usually because you don't want to hear what He has to say. It is much the same as when a spouse sneaks out and purchases something without consulting the other spouse. Often the one doesn't want the other to axe the purchase.

Wealth tends to create a prison that inevitably puffs up and isolates you from God and from others. In ancient Near Eastern cultures the elders of the city made up their minds in community.

Tellingly, the man in Jesus' parable has no audience for his speech. Could it be that his real poverty is his loneliness and emptiness of community? Would you know if your heart was a prisoner to greed?

Paul says that greed is idolatry. "Consider the members of your earthly body as dead to . . . greed, which amounts to idolatry" (Col. 3:5). Idolatry is living for anything in place of God, drawing life from the created rather than the Creator. Idolatry has at its heart unbelief: you really don't believe God can give you satisfaction; you do believe satisfaction comes from the things you desire. You don't believe, "Nothing I desire compares with you, Lord" (from Prov. 8:11). Perhaps that is simply because you aren't comparing the things you think will make you happy with the supreme desirability and beauty of the Lord. If you are miserable in your idolatry it is because God loves you and won't let you find peaceful happiness in it. Misery should lead you to repentance.

Idolatry is a plan.

Like each of us, the rich man has a plan to secure happiness. It seems to make perfectly good sense. Build better barns to store up the goods.

Do you agree with the premise of this chapter, that he is talking to the wrong person about money? But that's a symptom of a more critical problem: his soul has a false trust. "A rich man's wealth is his strong city, and like a high wall in his own imagination" (Prov. 18:11).

There is a fatal flaw in his plan. Money is his security for the future, but he hasn't looked far enough ahead. He's missing just one factor. An unexpected, sudden death. "But God said to him, 'You fool! This very night your soul is required of you; and now who will own what you have prepared?' " (Luke 12:20). The word "required" is commonly used for the return of a loan. Both his money and his soul are on loan from God.

Do you feel the weight of the separation? God will require your soul, but your wealth stays on earth. "We have brought nothing into the world, so we cannot take anything out of it either" (1 Tim. 6:7). All the stuff you loved and hoarded, gone in an instant. "Riches do not profit in the day of wrath . . . " (Prov. 11:4). Wealth will have no role in determining whether your soul is perfectly righteous for heaven, or whether you possess the shield of righteousness on judgment day. The penniless and the billionaire will stand as equals before God's wrath.

Do you see the nature of foolishness? Reasoning about life without reference to the God of life: not talking to God about His money; not talking to God about your soul; not talking to God about life and death.

Would he have lived differently if he knew? Knew what? Whatever he invested for himself he would never see again. Whatever he invested for God he would have for eternity. Jesus said, "Store up for yourselves treasures in heaven . . . " (Matt. 6:20). Whatever those treasures look like, they will not compare to the passing pleasure of wealth on earth.

Jesus warns that spiritual bankruptcy in this life produces eternal bankruptcy in the next. "So is the man who stores up treasure for himself, and is not rich toward God" (Luke 12:21). Jesus calls him a fool. There is a play on words here. In Greek, the word for the *good life* the man wants is *euphron*. Jesus calls him *aphron*, one of four Greek words for *fool*.

Foolishness believes it is all about me. It's all mine. My kingdom over the kingdom of God. If you invest only in you, you obviously don't believe in God; you are a practical atheist. Here's a great irony:

"Your Father has chosen gladly to give you the kingdom" (Luke 12:32). God gives the kingdom and eternal life as a gift!

Why must He? Because you can't buy your way into it--it's too costly. You don't deserve it, you can't earn it, you're not qualified. To see God you need moral wealth or the perfection of moral righteousness. Frankly, you and I are bankrupt. God knows that. You've got to get there through another man's riches.

There was a rich man who spoke to God about His wealth. He said one day, I want to set it all aside to seek another treasure. I want lost, greedy, selfish sinners to be in our family. So the Father sent Him out on a mission, not of greed but of love, to a harvest of human souls.

> *Although [Christ Jesus] existed in the form of God, [He] did not regard equality with God a thing to be grasped, but emptied Himself, taking the form of a bond-servant, and being made in the likeness of men. Being found in appearance as a man, he humbled Himself by becoming obedient to the point of death, even death on a cross.* (Phil. 2:6-8)

Jesus came to heal our hearts, to deliver from the insanity of living for things that are destined to perish. He came to set us free for love and generosity, and for finding God our greatest treasure. Jesus says, I will establish your value; wealth can't. When it's gone, what are you?

Has the harvest of Jesus' love come to you? You can tell by your faith.

Trust His promise to save you from your greed, idolatry, and all other sins, and receive the gift of the kingdom. Faith believes the word of promise: you are of great value to God! Faith will embolden you to spend your life for God's glory. True faith is always rich toward God. Faith measures giving not by how much you give, but by how much you give up. When His grace comes, He makes you like Himself. "For you know the grace of our Lord Jesus Christ, that though He was rich, yet for your sake He became poor, so that you through His poverty might become rich" (2 Cor. 8:9).

Faith enjoys talking to God about wealth. Faith trusts that God will lead you to the place of generous and wise investment. Faith frees you from anxiety, fear, jealousy, and discontentment. Faith knows that money can't buy the priceless value of the kingdom of God:

"For the kingdom of God is not eating and drinking, but righteousness and peace and joy in the Holy Spirit" (Romans 14:17).

Cooling Down a Hot Temper

He who is slow to anger has great understanding,
But he who is quick-tempered exalts folly. (Proverbs 14:29)

Recent archaeological studies have discovered a rare, ancient proverb, known in virtually all cultures of the world: "When mama ain't happy, ain't nobody happy." How true, yes? To be fair, I don't think this ditty is saying as much about mama as it is about the social effects of strong emotions, particularly anger. When someone is angry—whether daddy, brother, sister, or the boss--you know it, feel it, and have to work around it. It's like a fire; you have to be careful or someone's going to get burned. That's why Proverbs warns: "A *fool is arrogant and careless. A quick-tempered man acts foolishly*" (Prov. 14:16b-17a).

Anger can be explosive and lead you to places you shouldn't go: murder, jealousy, depression, and all kinds of personal and social ills. It can get you close to the heart of God or quench His Spirit in a heartbeat. Can you tell when someone is irritated? Of course! Anger is very hard to hide. It's one of the most visible emotions. I remember my high school football coach's inability to disguise his anger: red-faced, nostrils flared, fists clenched, voice raised. The Bible assumes we all get angry, but anger is an area of life with significant potential for stumbling:

A fool always loses his temper, but a wise man holds it back. (Prov. 29:11)

He who is slow to anger has great understanding, but he who is quick-tempered exalts folly. (Prov. 14:29)

He who restrains his words has knowledge, and he who has a cool spirit is a man of understanding. (Prov. 17:27)

What distinguishes the fool from the wise man? Outwardly we can usually tell the difference: one is hot and the other is cool. One is primed and ready for a fight, and the other is calm and collected. I know people who seem ready for a fight, and they're stinky to be around. Inwardly, what is the difference between the fool and the wise person? It isn't *whether* they get angry, but *how* they get angry. See the contrast: the fool is *quick*-tempered, the wise is *slow* to anger. Controlled anger defines moral strength: "He who is slow to anger is better than the mighty" (Prov. 16:32). The question for you, therefore, is, How do you become a *slow-to-anger* person?

These verses give us the answer: you have *great understanding.* The pathway out of destructive anger is knowledge, perspective, and truth in a biblical worldview. What four things does wisdom teach us that we need to understand about anger in order to become a slow-to-anger kind of person?

1. The history of anger

There are essentially two stages in the history of anger. In stage one, before the fall, anger is natural to God's good creation. How so? Anger is a part of God's character, though His is never capricious or ill-humored. "God is a righteous judge, and a God who has indignation every day" (Ps. 7:11). When He looks at evil His anger does not turn away:

"He who does not obey the Son will not see life, but the

wrath of God abides on him" (John 3:36). God wouldn't be good if He wasn't angry with wickedness, injustice, or whatever harms innocent, good things. People often hear of God's anger and want to impugn it. But consider the alternatives; no good person was ever indifferent to evil or condoning of it.

If God has righteous, appropriate anger, then Adam and Eve, as God's image-bearers, had it before they fell. When Satan came in to the Garden of Eden and lied about God and life and death, offering sin as an acceptable lifestyle, they should have been furious with righteous indignation and clubbed the serpent to death. They should have reacted with perfect anger--strong emotions, clear arguments, and violent action (Dave Powlison, *The Journal of Biblical Counseling*, Vol. 14, No.1 [Fall 1995] 46).

In stage two, our capacity for righteous anger became seriously spoiled at the fall. Humans fell under the dominion of Satan, the angriest person in the universe. His anger stems from his hatred of God and malice toward those who bear his image and serve him.

The essence of anger is: "I want my way, not God's, and because I can't have my way, I rage" (Powlison 42).

The result of sin entering the world is that we are fundamentally angry at the wrong person; we should be angry at the destroyer of God's good creation, Satan, but we're mad at God instead. When anger filled Cain's heart he went out and murdered his brother. Proverbs says we all have the spirit of angry Cain in us: "The foolishness of man ruins his way, and his heart rages against the Lord" (Prov. 19:3). "He who walks in his uprightness fears the Lord, but he who is devious in his ways despises Him" (Prov. 14:2).

So anger is part of our fallen character. Much of human anger is sinful. If you don't believe it, have children. There they are in all their sweetness, until they don't get their way. Then what? A "hissy fit," a burst of anger you most certainly didn't teach them. To compound that sad reality, we also learn anger. If you don't believe it, have children. As they get older they begin to imitate the ways in which their parents get angry. So: "Do not associate with a man given to anger, or go with a hot-tempered man, or you will learn his ways and find a snare for yourself" (Prov. 22:24).

Paul concurs in 1 Corinthians 15:33: " 'Bad company corrupts good morals.' "

2. The price of anger

Anger is an emotion affecting the whole person--body, mind, and motives—with tangible consequences.

a. It leads rapidly to relational meltdown and further strife.

"An angry man stirs up strife" (Prov. 29:22).

"The churning of anger produces strife" (Prov. 30:33).

b. Anger sticks with us, fostering more sin, until its grip is decisively broken.

"A man of great anger will bear the penalty, for if you rescue him, you will only have to do it again" (Prov. 19:19).

"A hot-tempered man abounds in transgression" (Prov. 29:22).

c. Anger alienates others.

"A quick-tempered man acts foolishly, and a man of evil devices is hated" (Prov. 14:17).

Why don't angry people have many friends? They aren't pleasant to be around. The cost? Angry people lose the blessing of benefiting from the gifts of others, and vice versa.

d. Uncontrolled anger rarely escapes some form of penalty.

"A man of great anger will bear the penalty" (Prov. 19:19).

When you go to purchase a major item--a car, house, appliance, or investment--you typically ask a lot of questions. Proverbs says the wise man stops and considers what his anger is worth. What does it achieve? Is the value of the outburst worth what you pay for it? Mark Cuban, owner of the Dallas Mavericks, has accumulated more than one million dollars in fines for criticizing the NBA officiating and its commissioner. Does he really think it's worth all that money?

Have you calculated the effect of your anger on your children? Your kids won't open their hearts to you because they fear you. The unresolved resentment you hold against your spouse, is it worth the fruit of it--lack of intimacy, joy, and the experience of kindness and oneness? No wonder Paul warns, "Be angry and yet do not sin; do not let the sun go down on your anger" (Eph. 4:26).

3. The cause of anger

Dave Powlison (*The Journal of Biblical Counseling*, Vol. 14, No. 2 [1995] 12f) explains that we often entertain two misunderstandings about the source of anger. First, we tend to think anger is like a radiator inside us. Given enough provocation, anger builds up and releases under pressure. It's better to see anger as something you do, a judgment you make against a perceived wrong that plays out in the mind. For example, when I drive on vacation, it seems to never fail. After traveling 260 miles toward our rental beach cottage on a four-lane highway, I get behind a slowpoke going six miles per hour under the speed limit on a winding, single lane road for the last four miles. God seems to test my patience along this stretch of road--without exception. And I fail. I rage. I become investigator—prosecuting attorney—witness—judge—jury—jailor—hangman. Anger is an attitude of judgment: "I don't approve of this slow driver"; a condemnation: "cursed be the idiot causing me inconvenience"; and displeasure: "so I rage as a result."

Therefore, anger is something you do:

Feeling→intense   thinking→vivid   imagining→clear judgments→behavior (usually tongue first)

A second misunderstanding is that the source of anger is "out there": the problem is my spouse, roommate, professor, neighbor's incessantly barking dog, child, putter, boss, car . . . whatever. It's better to see anger in terms of goals and beliefs. When you're angry, ask yourself, What is it I want so badly? What am I demanding right now that I think I so desperately need in order to be happy? What goal am I pursuing that is being blocked?

ME-------/-----→GOAL

/ (Anger comes from blocked goals)

You need to ask the Spirit to show you what selfish

110

cravings are ruling your heart, what you've enthroned as a must-have: control, approval, mastery, peace, leisure, success, pleasure, wealth, reputation, etc. Back to driving behind a slowpoke . . . is your goal not to be late? Superficially it is. But what's driving that goal (excuse the pun)? There are deeper goals, such as being late makes you look bad. You don't want to look bad because then people may not like you. See the real goal? You need approval to feel intact as a human being.

Your demands reveal what you believe. Sinful anger always believes lies about God. God exists to give me what I want. God's not fixing this because He doesn't love me. But honestly, is that the limit of your understanding? Why haven't you considered that God is trying to teach you something? Maybe God is giving you an opportunity to become a different kind of person. Maybe God is exposing your self-dependence so you can learn to pray, or lean on others. Maybe your children are frustrating you so God can picture for you the way He sees *your* heart. Maybe your life isn't as calm as you want it so God can forge true faith in you, and get you closer to the heart of Jesus, who didn't have a calm life.

If you want to control your anger, you need to learn to distinguish between desires and needs. Often we get angry when we turn our desires into our needs. It's one thing to *desire* that your children obey you, but you don't *need* that to be humanly intact. It's one thing to *desire* respect from another person, but you don't *need* that to be whole spiritually. What you *need* to be whole spiritually, you already have, if you possess the riches of Christ, the benefits of the gospel. And what wisdom you may lack, God will give to you when you depend on Him.

So you desire to look competent, be heard, be valued, or seen as knowledgeable, skilled, or mature in front of others? Why do you need to be valued, heard, or seen as important? Don't make that a goal—something you must have to feel complete as a person. Why should you abandon that as a goal? It isn't something God says you must have to be happy, godly, or peaceful. It might be nice to have it but you don't need it to be godly. Plus, achieving that goal requires the cooperation of others, and you simply can't control that.

But you maintain that it's wrong for others to insult you. That's their problem. God hasn't called any of us to an insult-free life. You're called to give blessings, not to expect them or to receive them. So how do you respond to insults or neglect? Sinful anger answers with pride: How dare you! You're the jerk! I demand respect! Godly anger enthrones Jesus. Jesus says, "Forgive them; for they do not know what they are doing" (Luke 23:34). Such a response to anger or ill-treatment clothes you in true moral beauty. "A man's discretion makes him slow to anger, and it is his glory to overlook a transgression" (Prov. 19:11). "A fool's anger is known at once, but a prudent man conceals dishonor" (Prov. 12:16).

How do you overlook or look beyond an insult? Put the cross between you and the insulter. The cross has already criticized you—far worse than any human being could. Next time say, "If you really knew me you'd say worse!" Godly anger never needs to win or to be proven right. Paul says, "Why not rather be wronged" (1 Cor. 6:7). You will gain understanding by talking less and listening more, lest you become angry before you know the whole story. Set your opinions aside and open your mind. "Everyone must be quick to hear, slow to speak, and slow to anger . . ." (James 1:19).

4. God's anger

You are ultimately powerless to become a slow-to-anger person until you experience God's anger. How? First, you experience God's anger in mercy. The wrath your sins deserved fell upon Jesus on the cross. The bow of His anger was drawn back on you, but released into the heart of righteous Jesus. He took it all; there's none left for you. God forgives and changes angry people by revealing to them that His anger is spent at the cross. Second, you experience God's anger in deliverance. Through the gospel God has poured out His Spirit into our hearts to be a burning fire against our sinful anger because He knows how bad it is for us and for the unity of the body of Christ. He won't tolerate sin in us, and helps us hate our sin. Instead of being mad *as* hell, be mad *at* hell; turn your anger on the devil and your own sin. Do you hate it more than others' sins? The evidence you don't is how long you entertain negative thoughts about others. You ought to pray for yourself the way you would pray for others' frailties. Humility throws water on the fire of anger.

Third, you experience God's anger in hope. Our sure confidence, future certainty, God-sworn expectation, is that at the Day of the Lord—Judgment Day—God in His anger will fulfill His promises to alleviate all injustice, suffering, sickness, pain, sorrow, and loss, and to destroy His enemies, including death and the powers of evil. The larger you magnify God's mercy, deliverance, and hope, the smaller become your reasons for anger.

Case Study: Expectation and Anger

I have been very zealous for the Lord, the God of hosts; for the sons of Israel have forsaken Thy covenant, torn down Thine altars and killed the prophets with the sword. And I alone am left; and they seek my life to take it away." (1 Kings 19:10)

When I was in the second grade my family moved to Richmond, VA. Someone told my mom that a local toy store welcomed new kids to town with a free toy. I'll never forget the excitement and anticipation of getting a new toy. I imagined going to the Matchbox cars and picking out several I'd always wanted (they sold for only $.49 each in 1964), or maybe finding a cowboy gun and holster. We arrived at the store and to our deep chagrin we were handed these hard, fuzzy little piggy banks. How disappointing! From that day forward whenever we drove past that store my brothers and I made disparaging remarks about the worthless toys we were given which fell far below our expectations.

Yes, as young boys we were disappointed, but on a very small scale. Let's up the ante. Do you wonder how many of us would confess our disenchantment with life, or perhaps more honestly, with God, because He didn't meet our expectations? Whether expectations about marriage, children, a ministry, or a job, have you have essentially given up a course you started for the Lord because you didn't see the results you expected? If we know anything about history we know that God's people of all ages have suffered under weakened faith- when expectations didn't comport with reality.

If that is true, how do we maintain faith when God seems to do the opposite of what we expect? What do you do when you lose your sense of purpose- or more importantly- what does God do? The story recorded in 1 Kings 19:1-18 answers that question. What the story reveals is shockingly honest. Elijah had lost his sense of purpose. After all, he is a super star, a spiritual giant. When God chooses the two weightiest OT characters to appear with Jesus on the Mount of Transfiguration, it's Moses and Elijah. He is Mr. Spiritual, prophet of the highest regard; he is to authentic religion what Tiger Woods is to golf. But…he's suicidal. The text makes no effort to hide his despondency and despair. Why? For our benefit: so we know how to maintain faith when God doesn't meet our expectations.

Why is Elijah depressed?

Elijah just finished the lead role in one of the greatest miracles ever recorded, the fire which fell from heaven at Mt. Carmel. God had triumphed, He mocked His enemies, and Elijah put the sword to the false prophets of Baal. It was a holy adrenaline rush of the tallest order. He was filled with faith, and God used him mightily. He had no doubt God was in control, was all powerful, and was drawing the hearts of His people again. He prayed for rain and it came. He called fire down from heaven, and it fell.

Elijah loves his country, he loves the God of Israel, and now there's hope. People will turn back to God. Didn't they see the fire lick up the water and then fall on their faces saying, "The LORD He is God!"? Rain returned to the land. Revival is on the way. Any minute Elijah would hear the report: Ahab is repenting; he is relinquishing his wicked stronghold on the nation; Jezebel wants to confess her sins and trust Yahweh. Yes, sir, here comes Jezebel's messenger now.

She what? She wants to kill me? You have GOT to be

kidding? Nothing's changed. I don't understand, Lord. Isn't a revival guaranteed to follow such a display of divine power?

So Elijah fearfully runs for his life to Beersheba, the southernmost city in the land, where he'd be safe. He falls to the ground, energy draining from his body as all hope spills from his heart. He is spent- emotionally, physically, and spiritually. It is as exhausting dealing with evil as it is not seeing it relent. Elijah leaves his servant: we're going out of business, I've had enough. He lays down a solitary man under a lone broom tree: *"Lord, take my life."* If Mt. Carmel won't get results, nothing will.

Can you imagine the swing in emotion? One day he is brimming with confidence and faith, the next day he is totally deflated. When zeal gives way to despair, invariably we wonder: "God, who are you?"

Even so, there's a sense in which Elijah's despondency is so refreshing. If God won't move he doesn't want to live. Moses experienced the exact same despair, as did John the Baptist. There's something good about that. He is highly invested in the welfare of Israel and God's glory. He hates evil. Do you see, therefore, how Elijah's despair is not primarily in response to his circumstances, but rather with respect to his expectations?

Think about the possible ways he could have responded:

1) If he thoroughly left the results to God- I'll be obedient to God, the rest is up to Him- why be upset?
2) If he didn't care what happened, a detached "que sera sera" attitude toward life, he wouldn't be so despondent.
3) If he was an overachiever/workaholic, he'd have said, OK, that didn't seem to work, what's next, Lord? Give me my next assignment right now!

I wonder how many of us are content to merely carry on

with God outside of the picture. What's the evidence that may be you? Look at your prayer life: Are you asking God to do things three weeks out? What have you celebrated with God about recently? What is the tenor of your worship? Is there concrete evidence in your life that you live by hope?

So Elijah wants to die because God has not met his expectations. End of story? Hardly.

What does God do?

In summary, He tenderly provides for Elijah, giving him exactly what he needs. And you need to know that, too. God knows what you need; He will give it to you. He is compassionate and generous, protective and wise. Our guarantee? The Father gave us His Son!
"He who did not spare his own son, but gave him up for us all, how will he not also with him freely give us all things?" (Rom.8:32) See how Paul reasons from the greater to the lesser? If you need a $1000, and someone gives you $50,000, it logically follows that there is ample money for what you need. Is the God and Father of our Lord Jesus Christ an "ample grace" God abundantly sufficient for all our needs? There is not a shred of evidence in the Bible that He is anything but that.

a)   God comes to Elijah.

He comes in the Angel of the Lord. Sometimes in the OT that is an angel, other times it is the Lord Jesus Christ in a pre-incarnation theophany. The Angel of the Lord does the Lord's bidding. In this case...
...the Angel gives Elijah a lecture?
...He berates him because of his sin?
...He does a spiritual inventory exploring the reasons for his depression?
No. He gives him food. Sometimes we just need food. He allows him to continue to nap. Sometimes we just need to

118

sleep. We live in a physical universe. Sometimes you may need medication. The angel touches Elijah; sometimes we need a hug. Here's some more food; that's serious food because it lasts 40 days. These tender provisions are pictures of the sustaining grace lavished upon God's children in the Bread of Life.

b) God probes Elijah's heart.

Depression isn't just a physical problem, nor is it simply a spiritual problem. Elijah heads to Mt Horeb. God meets him and asks, *"Why are you here?"* Now that's not for God's benefit, but for Elijah's. I wonder if God is getting Elijah to look beyond his circumstances:
"Yes, you should expect great things from me, but you can't dictate the timeline."
"Elijah, you were faithful at Mt Carmel, and that's enough; I control the results."
"Yes, I used you to perform a great miracle, but don't nourish your faith simply on that. Don't insist that the spectacular sustain you. My promises are meant to carry you in the ordinary."

What is God's goal in asking, *Why are you here?* He's getting to the root of depression. It is an occasion to see the heart, and to listen carefully to it. I'm not sure Elijah hears his own heart, but we do, in his words:
I have been very zealous for the Lord, the God of hosts; for the sons of Israel have forsaken Thy covenant, torn down Thine altars and killed the prophets with the sword. And I alone am left; and they seek my life to take it away." (1 Kings 19:10)

Commentators are not agreed on the exact sentiment behind Elijah's words. It may be he is simply heartbroken over the apostasy of his nation. Or it may be, I did all this for God, I'm the only one left, poor, poor, pitiful me. Assuming the latter, what do his words reveal about his heart? God's *Why* gets at what he is demanding of life events or God.

Ed Welch explains in his book <u>Depression: A Stubborn Darkness</u>, when you listen to your heart, you need to listen through the stethoscope of Biblical truth. When you do you hear two pulses:

One, there are fundamentally two ways to live:

Do you love God or something else?
Do you trust, worship, serve, obey, treasure, seek the glory of, God or something else?

Our hearts naturally set affections on the wrong things. We are self-reliant and self-serving. As Ed Welch writes, "you are immensely loyal to your interpretation of yourself and your world." (p.129)

Two, we are creatures with needs and desires and we want to indulge them.

I want, I want is the cry of the soul. We want more love, freedom, control, approval, pleasure, money, sex, leisure, peace, however you fill in the blank.
Do you know the problem with that? On the one hand, it is declaring that God is not enough. On the other, no matter how much of our wants we get, they will never satisfy us. When you feel empty, therefore, it is usually a sign that you are putting trust in something that can never sustain you. You were created to trust God while enjoying the good things He gives, without making them the center of your life.

Dr. Welch explains how idolatry grows in our hearts. We want things and we aren't sure God will give them to us, so we put our trust in other gods. This is the problem of the human heart- misplaced trust. When you dig deep into anger you find it is about spiritually allegiances. Whom will you trust? "We value, love and trust something in creation more than the Creator, and since there is nothing in creation that is intended

to bear the weight of our trust, we are bound to live in fear."
Do you feel how sickening that is? Although God has
promised to give us the kingdom, the kingdom doesn't sound
so great. (p.149)

Apply this to Elijah. Elijah starts in fear because Jezebel
has promised to kill him. That threat is legitimate to fear. But
in fleeing, his fear turns to anger, which simmers to depression.
Ed Welch counsels, "the wisest way to approach depression is
to assume you are angry." But anger hides. We are often the
last person to see it. You can have hot, explosive anger at one
end of the spectrum, or cold, withdrawn anger at the other,
manifested in sullenness and self-pity.

Is Elijah angry? It seems so. His protest seems to be a self-
righteous, I did everything you asked me to do. I'm right! I
don't deserve this! Why is this happening to me?

Ed Welch provides this gauge to see if your anger is right
or wrong:
Does your anger act to condemn or to help?
Most of our anger is with other people- they let you down- a
spouse, friend, relative, co-worker, or pastor. In anger are you
moving in condemnation or redemption? Do you want
retaliation or to forgive and act to help those who disappoint
you?

In the end what does Elijah need? The same thing you
need when you're depressed: more clothes, a new car, a better
spouse, another CD, junk food…No. Elijah needs to hear the
word of God.

On what do you nourish your faith? Where is your faith
being exercised? Faith is not a cell phone worn on your hip, to
be used when needed. It is more of a muscle either exercised
consistently and therefore strengthening, or left to atrophy and
therefore weakening. Elijah wanted to see a revival, a good
desire; God wanted him to live for His glory, a better goal.

Do you see how liberating that is? Living for God's glory, versus living for results. If Elijah is first about God's glory, then he lives with the results and presses on. This is revealed clearly in the thinking of one of my favorite bands, Switchfoot: *"We aren't trying to be everyone's favorite band. We're trying to pursue an audience of one, essentially.* [What is that?] *The longer we're been a band, the more we're not in it just to make other people give us their stamp of approval. There has to be a greater purpose than just making people applaud for what we're doing, and as long as we're convinced we're exactly where God has us at the moment, that has to be the ultimate goal.*

c)   God reveals His grace.

In spite of his weak faith, God won't let Elijah go. Elijah needs to learn afresh that you can't struggle with evil without the assurance of God's grace. What is the evidence of that in Elijah? He goes to Horeb. He needs revelation. He wants to see God. It's the same place Moses went in Ex.34 when he desperately needed to see God. God asks twice, *"What are you doing here?"* Elijah answers identically each time. *I've been zealous, I'm the only one left.* In other words, what are you doing God?

What is God's answer? Come here and stand before Me. God sends a strong wind, then an earthquake, then a fire. But God isn't in those. Then comes a gentle blowing, literally, "the sound of gentle quietness". God is saying, "I can come in power if I want to. I've revealed Myself in those forms before and I will again.   I can show up in many forms. But Elijah, you've put me in a box. My will is much larger than any of your notions of what I might be up to. You may want fire but get a whisper; you may want a whisper but get fire. Either way, be assured of this: I will give you grace. You can't fight evil without the assurance of grace."

God hid Elijah in the cave because the wind, fire and earthquake- all forms of judgment in the Bible- would have consumed him. Elijah isn't touched by the fury of God's judgment because of the rock. The rock took the judgment.

Jesus stood before the fire, wind, and earthquake of God's wrath for you. Elijah finally saw the rock in which he'd been hidden when he saw the glory of Christ on the Mount of Transfiguration.

d) God gives Elijah a new task

God tells Elijah to go, return to Damascus and anoint a pagan king. What does this mean? God's still at work. A judgment will come in due time. He will ultimately deal with wicked kings in His perfect time. And Elijah, by the way, I've still got 7000 faithful ones in Israel. You aren't alone.

By grace God shows Elijah the same truths we need to understand:

1. Elijah, you can't give your life for the sins of Israel, nor can you confront evil alone. Only God's perfect Son can confront evil alone and lay down his life as a righteous substitute for the sins of God's people.

2. You don't see the whole picture. When you look out of the window on an airplane while it's landing, you assume the pilot with the full view clearly sees the runway. In the same way, we can trust the One who does. And if you don't see the whole picture, it just may be that your version of Christianity is not the only one. Could it be you could learn from others who aren't exactly like you?

3. Evil will be with us until Jesus comes again. He'll deal evil its final blow. It's your responsibility to foster no friendship with the values of a world under judgment, but rather, garner enduring friendships with fellow believers.

Sloth: Enemy of Life

*I passed by the field of the sluggard and by the
vineyard of the man lacking sense, and behold, it was
completely overgrown with thistles; its surface was
covered with nettles, and its stone wall was broken down.
When I saw, I reflected upon it; I looked and received
instruction. "A little sleep, a little slumber, a little folding
of the hands to rest," then your poverty will come as a
robber, and your want like an armed man. (Prov. 24:30-
34)*

A father and son are taking a walk around the block. They
stop and stare at their neighbor's farm.

"Daddy, why is that man's garden so messy? Why is his
stone wall falling down?"

"Son, do you ever see him working it?"

"No, Daddy, and we walk by here all the time."

There it is, in all its inglorious disarray—the field of the
sluggard—painfully obvious for all to see. It silently screams
neglect: wasteful, tragic, unnecessary, and inexcusable.

This Scripture is vintage Proverbs. By observation, either
by the ear or by the eye, by comparison and then reflection, we
learn that certain principles woven into the fabric of life by the

Creator cannot be broken with impunity. There is a reason the wall is falling over, and there are serious consequences. See the connections?

sleep→neglect→disarray→poverty

Is laziness a source of stumbling for you? Your answer may depend on how you measure it. Busyness is not the opposite of sloth, or the antidote. You can be busy and still be lazy. I suspect many folks in the professional ranks oscillate between frenzy and collapse. Sloth is a failure to do what God has called you to do. It is an indifference to the priorities of a godly life. Busyness may mask sloth for a time, but it is not virtue, especially if the pricetag is failure to fulfill your basic commitments to the Lord. That's the main concern of Proverbs: setting you free to understand how life works, how to avoid the stumbling blocks common to us all, with the result that you have joy living for the Lord. None of us has an excuse, because God has given every one of us enough time in each day to be faithfully obedient to Him.

Sloth may not be an all-or-nothing matter for you. You may be industrious at work, but lazy toward your spouse, or kids, or home, or church, or personal finances, or health. But any form of sloth is sin. Proverbs helps us understand it so God can set us free from its seductive pull.

The Cycle of Sloth

If you took a picture of sloth in the animal world, you'd see a tropical mammal that lives hanging upside-down, crawls ten feet per minute, sleeps 15-22 hours per day, and only eats what is in its immediate proximity. Proverbs paints a vivid picture of sloth in the human world; one thing tends to breed another:

The sluggard starts with excuses:

126

"The sluggard says, 'There is a lion outside; I will be killed in the streets!'" (Prov. 22:13).

He then pursues vain goals:

"He who tills his land will have plenty of bread, but he who pursues worthless things lacks sense" (Prov. 12:11).

He then rationalizes:

"The sluggard is wiser in his own eyes than seven men who can give a discreet answer" (Prov. 26:16).

Restlessness results from inactivity:

"The soul of the sluggard craves and gets nothing, but the soul of the diligent is made fat" (Prov. 13:4).

Constant obstacles plague his way:

"The way of the lazy is as a hedge of thorns, but the path of the upright is a highway" (Prov. 15:19).

He becomes irritating to others:

"Like vinegar to the teeth and smoke to the eyes, so is the lazy one to those who send him" (Prov. 10:26).

His laziness spells destruction:

"He also who is slack in his work is brother to him who destroys" (Prov. 18:9).

Slavery results as the ironic opposite of the easy street he wants:

"The hand of the diligent will rule, but the slack hand will be put to forced labor" (Prov. 12:24).

Why does God condemn sloth so strongly? We need only look to the parable of the talents in the teaching of Jesus to feel God's wrath: to the steward who did nothing, God says, "You wicked, lazy slave . . . " (Matt. 25:26). Two reasons stand out. First, sloth gobbles up life as God intended it. It's mockingly portrayed in the absurd: "The sluggard buries his hand in the dish, but will not even bring it back to his mouth" (Prov. 19:24). "A lazy man does not roast his prey" (Prov. 12:27). Second, because sloth is so unlike God. He upholds His creation; He stoops down to serve his people; He provides, and governs. He fulfills His obligations and keeps covenant, even when we don't. Where the sloth avoids pain at all costs, God in His Son went to the pain of all costs to redeem us from our sins.

The symptoms of sloth

1. The most visible symptom comes from the text. The astute observer received instruction by overhearing the sloth's little ditty:

"A little sleep, a little slumber, a little folding of the hands to rest" (Prov. 24:33).

According to scholar Derek Kidner, lazy people enjoy their delicious sleep too much. Sleep apparently is a narcotic to ease the pain of living in the real world. Their sleep is an escape, a refusal to face responsibility. Consequently, "opportunity slips away inches by minutes by the smallness of his surrenders" (Derek Kidner, _Proverbs_ [Leicester, England: Tyndale, 1964],

42).

"How long will you lie down, O sluggard? When will you arise from your sleep?" (Prov. 6:9).

"As the door turns on its hinges, so does the sluggard on his bed" (Prov. 26:14).

"Laziness casts into a deep sleep, and an idle man will suffer hunger" (Prov. 19:15).

Notice how laziness is its own judgment. The more you rest, the more you want to do so. Laziness casts a spell, as it were, on the soul, choking out ambition and industry. Apparently, one force to awaken sloth from its destructive trajectory is hunger.

2. Some commentators see in this repetition of the phrase "a little," "a little" an attitude toward life that responds to the question When? with, Some time. The sloth won't commit, surrenders too easily, and exerts only minimum effort, as revealed in Proverbs 20:4:

"The sluggard does not plow after the autumn, so he begs during the harvest and has nothing."

3. Excessive use of entertainment is also a symptom of sloth. This is yet another escape into a world where we have no responsibility and no consequences to our actions.

4. Busyness may be another form of sloth, a cover-up for a failure to do what is important. You may have tons of activity in your life, may be task-driven, but may use that as an excuse to feel good about yourself, when you really don't love people or God well.

5. Relativism: Sloth is not simply idleness of body. It can also be idleness of mind, disguised as a virtue, tolerance. Tolerance in our culture usually means, Don't judge anyone else's point of view. "I won't challenge you if you don't challenge me." But that may simply be a mask on a refusal to do the hard work of critical thinking to determine good and evil. When postmodernism claims that everyone's viewpoint is legitimate, that may just be, according to J. J. Reno, "a protective dogma designed to fend off any power that might claim our loyalty." We may be lazy in our thinking in order to insulate ourselves from "the sober potency of arguments, and the force of evidences, from the rightful claims of reason and the wisdom of the past." To say, "I refuse to take a stand," may be mere intellectual sloth.

The same could be said of aesthetics. In the name of individual expression, subjectivism gobbles up standards of truth and beauty.

The diagnosis

There are two verses that help us understand what is driving sloth in the heart:

"The soul of the sluggard craves and gets nothing" (Prov. 13:4).

This first verse tells us that sloth is not absence of desire, but the failure to act. This person claims, "I'm going to be rich one day," but never gets off his butt.

"He who tills his land will have plenty of bread, but he who pursues worthless things lacks sense" (Prov. 12:11).

This person has pursuit, but desires something that is empty because of a laziness of focus or vision. Everyone's heart pursues something. Even the person who chooses to do very little is motivated by a desire for relaxation or disengagement from life. The question is, Why? What is driving a heart that refuses to seek God's will? What is distasteful about God's will that we find it unworthy of our wholehearted pursuit?

If sloth is a refusal to face the world, an escape from reality in whatever form, then sloth is motivated by fear: fear of pain or hurt; fear of failure, rejection, looking bad, being found out, losing control; fear of stepping outside what you deem your comfort zone or place of security. The sluggard's fear is exposed in the almost comical excuse, "There is a lion outside; I will be killed in the streets" (Prov. 22:13).

To unmask sloth, deconstruct your fears. Why is that lion in the street the worst thing that could happen to you? Is the pain of failure, for example, so unbearable that you refuse to risk? Is the pain of rejection so bad that you refuse to love? If you give your all and prove to be average, is that so horrible? What are you saying about God? That He has left you all alone, that you are an orphan in this mean world, with no defense or security? You've denied God's Fatherly providence, the assurance that He's always working in all situations for your good, and you've regarded His promises as empty.

When you distrust God's promises you invariably trust yourself. Full of self-absorption, you think everything is always about you, and when it is, you are terrorized by your own fears. Do you really find this the most satisfying way to live? Are you suffering under the weight of your small ambitions? Your self-trust, no-faith approach to life is self-defeating. It's more painful than failing and allowing God to pick you up. One way to measure this is in your fellowship. Are you slothful toward sharing your life with other believers?

If so, you rob yourself of full humanity (found in loving and serving others) and you rob others of whatever spiritual equity God has given you to share with them.

The Cure

What could move you to risk your safe world to attempt something greater than yourself? Is there a power on earth that can change your heart to say, "I delight to do Your will" (Ps. 40:8)? There is a man who said that, without one ounce of sloth in His soul: Jesus. He said it under the most difficult and fearful of circumstances. What did He possess that we lack, which drove Him to the most extreme measures of complicity with God's will—dying on the cross? Perhaps the answer is in John 8:29: "I always do the things that are pleasing to [the Father]." He had a Father, a friend if you will, whom it would be unthinkable to disappoint. If you think God is an ogre, of course you'll have reasons to resist his will. But if He is good, gracious, and a friend who sticks closer than a brother, you'll do anything for him. "If God is for us, who is against us?" (Rom. 8:31).

The gospel answers our worst fears. You'll never be rejected, you are perfectly loved, and you have enormous significance. Jesus has faced your worst fear for you--rejection by God--and set you free to fail in the arms of a gracious Father. Perfect love casts out fear. There is no reprisal with God for admitting your sins and fears. He knows your sloth without condemnation and with compassion, if you are in Christ. He is a thousand times more kind than the parent who picks up a child after a fall.

Self-Control

He who is slow to anger is better than the mighty,
And he who rules his spirit, than he who captures a city.
(Prov. 16:32)

Years ago, I played pickup basketball on a regular basis at the university near my home in Fort Worth. I had very simple goals: get exercise, don't get hurt, and maintain a good testimony by my sportsmanship.

One day I was getting hacked repeatedly around the basket, and I lost it. After one too many chops on my forearms, I threw the ball to the floor as hard as I could in a fit of rage. Everyone stood stunned for a moment. They knew I was a preacher. They'd never heard me talk trash, use profanity, play dirty, or lose my cool. The moment I threw the ball down I knew I compromised my witness. Immediately I wanted to explain myself, "Guys, you know that's not really me!" But what's the truth? That *was* the real me, given enough provocation. I lost self-control. The walls of restraint and propriety vanished from my mind at that moment. I acted impulsively out of my greatest desire at that instant. My goal to be a godly example was swallowed up by a more powerful goal, to display my outrage at being hacked so much.

Proverbs wants us to see that self-control is a wisdom issue that reveals your true strength, the real moral fiber of your heart, the ultimate god to which you bow down.

"He who is slow to anger is better than the mighty, and he who rules his spirit, than he who captures a city" (Prov. 16:32).

When you rule your spirit, you are stronger than the very best military operation the world has ever seen. Do you believe that? Do you really think that you are strongest when you are most under control? Proverbs seeks to demonstrate how this virtue applies in all areas of life:

1. It's true economically:

"He who loves pleasure will become a poor man; he who loves wine and oil will not become rich" (Prov. 21:17).

2. It's true physically:

"Have you found honey? Eat only what you need, that you not have it in excess and vomit it" (Prov. 25:16).

3. It's true socially:

"When you sit down to dine with a ruler, consider carefully what is before you, and put a knife to your throat if you are a man of great appetite" (Prov. 23:1-2).

Most important of all,

4. It's true spiritually:

"Like a city that is broken into and without walls is a man who has no control over his spirit" (Prov. 25:28).

The wall-less city is a powerful and provocative image. Everyone in ancient cultures understood the critical nature of city walls. They provided protection and safety for the city while securing an advantageous position against the enemy. How would you feel if you went on a four-day business or hunting trip, only to return to see your city walls crumbled to the ground? You'd be in terror for the welfare of your family, friends, business, and spiritual community. Are you in as much horror for your soul when you lose self-control? What does it mean that the walls of the city are broken down? It indicates the city is defenseless and therefore susceptible to attackers and plunderers; has lost its identity, being overrun and ruled by strangers; and has lost civility and order. A wall-less city is in chaos; when good, helpful rule is demolished, anarchy rules, and all that remains is for a tyrant to come to power.

When you lose self-control, which tyrant comes to power in your wall-less heart? Marauders of money? Scavengers of self-pity? Pirates of sensuality? If you can't think of anything, maybe your pride is out of control.

What is self-control?

Self-control is the ability to choose the most important thing over the urgent. It is the wisdom to be ruled by principle versus feelings or impressions or appearances. It employs ethical sight to determine what is best for your soul at all times, rather than what might seem good at any given time. Self-control is the inner fortitude to choose the godly goal and abandon anything else competing with it. When you lose self-control, you always settle for less than the best.

Self-control may be active--doing what you shouldn't do (losing your temper, exploding at another person, throwing your golf club, eating too much). Or it may be or passive--not doing what you should do (spending more time watching TV than playing with your children, reading the paper when you should read your Bible, playing with the car radio instead of looking at the road).

Why is self-control such a struggle?

We find the answer in the same chapter of the Bible,

Galatians 5, that tells us self-control is one of the nine fruit of the Holy Spirit. When your life is under God's control, nine fruit are evident, the last listed being self-control, perhaps because it is last to come to maturity in the Christian life. Galatians 5:16f explains how a war is raging inside us:

"But I say, walk by the Spirit, and you will not carry out the desire of the flesh. For the flesh sets its desire against the Spirit, and the Spirit against the flesh; for these are in opposition to one another, so that you may not do the things that you please."

Notice how many of these fruit of the flesh involve a loss of self-control: outbursts of anger, drunkenness, carousings, disputes, dissentions, sensuality . . . . This means whenever you desire to do the right thing, there is inevitably a competing urge waiting to rear its head. Not an ugly head, either, as sin usually presents its best face. Sin appears desirable and feels reasonable. Thankfully, self-control can see through the guise.

How do we grow in this grace?

How do we get the strength we desire for self-control? Look again at this image from Proverbs 25:28:

"Like a city that is broken into and without walls is a man who has no control over his spirit" Wisdom says to think of your heart as a city. Three questions arise from the image:

1. Who is king in the city? Who rules your heart?

We live in a culture that advocates ruling yourself as virtue:

136

"Be true to yourself, to your beliefs, however you fashion them. No one can tell you what is best for you. You must decide for yourself what you will value, what you will do with your life, who you want to love, etc."

In other words, be your own god. This explains the enormous proliferation of designer religions. When you pick and choose the way you want your spirituality, you're really establishing a little kingdom where you are God. If you've fashioned God in your own image, then effectively you control God. This has been the driving compulsion of the heart of man since the first sin in Eden.

Do you see any problems here? First, if there is a God who stands outside human making, you're on a collision course with Him. He doesn't give you the right to fashion myths about Him any more than I have a right to fashion myths about your character. Second, whatever you live for becomes your master. The Bible acknowledges the desire in the heart of man to be God, against all the compelling evidence that we are not. It's not hard to see, for example, how creaturely we are, how dependent and vulnerable we are as creatures:

* You can see only 180 degrees in front of you.

* You have to sleep and are completely defenseless when you do.

* You need breath, but can't make yourself breathe.

* How long could you live if you had no air, water, food?

* Who could survive on his or her own the first four years of life?

* Who could survive a minute if the sun blew up?

Our dependence is written all over our existence.

Being so vulnerable, are you fit to be king over your life?

The Bible says no. You need a power not of yourself. What does your knowledge of right and wrong do for you when passion rules your heart? When people mess up, it's invariably not for lack of understanding what is right. Look at what your loss of self-control has gotten you (economic hardship, relational meltdown, physical problems). You're a slave to your selfishness, lusts, food cravings, entertainments, money, and feelings. You do things you don't want other people to do to you.

King David in ancient Israel is a perfect example. If anyone would be regarded as free, it was the king; he could do whatever he wanted to do. Everyone answered to him. But even though he knew thoroughly the law of God, it had no power to restrain his lusts, urge to lie, or decision to kill one of his soldiers.

Christians believe in a king who will rule you better than you rule yourself. Where Jesus is King, there is freedom. Whatever you think is king over your heart, compare it with Jesus: He'll never abuse you, He is always just, He'll love you unconditionally, He has the power to always give you what you need, He can control your worst impulses. He rules you in such a way that you won't feel oppressed, but liberated. He is gracious and forgiving, more so than you forgive yourself. He frees you from a prison of self-protection so you can experience the joy of serving others. What a King! And His kingdom is forever. Do you know how to recognize His subjects?

His subjects will do anything for Him. But why? Through blind obedience? No way. Because He has done the unthinkable for them. Wonder of wonders, He lays down His life for those who love Him least! He takes your hatred of God, bears it in His body, and returns love for it. The perfect master of self-control, the only man who always made the right choice in every situation, offered Himself to a holy God as a sacrifice to pay for the sins of any who desire His salvation. Jesus did this by allowing the impregnable walls of His obedience, the walls of safety that surrounded Him, to be crushed to the ground by the just judgment of God for your sins. "Christ also died for sins once for all, the just for the unjust, so that he might bring us to God . . . " (1 Peter 3:18). Have you surrendered to King Jesus? Have you said, Come in, take your rightful place on the throne of my heart?

2. How does the king rule the city?

He takes control by the power of His Spirit. Helpful here is Paul's command in Ephesians 5:18, "Be filled with the Spirit." (See Michael Sharrett, *Watching Over the Heart* [Narrows VA: Metokos Press, 2005], 175-81, for fuller treatment of this theme.) If space allowed, we would explore the Reformed doctrine of the Spirit working with the Word.

3. How does the Spirit keep your heart strong?

Self-control is a function of what rules your mind. Therefore, what protects your mind, or captures your imagination, must be truth. When something other than the truth is ruling your mind, you're out of control. So think of the walls of the city of your mind as being only as strong as they are founded on the truth. Three simple principles follow:

Principle #1: Don't believe everything you tell yourself.

"Do not be conformed to this world, but be transformed by the renewing of your mind" (Rom. 12:2).

Principle #2: Challenge your thoughts as to their veracity

and truthfulness.

"We are destroying speculations and every lofty thing raised up against the knowledge of God, and we are taking every thought captive to the obedience of Christ" (2 Cor. 10:5).

Principle #3:   Become so well-acquainted with God's Word that you begin to think with increasing conformity to it.

"If you continue in My word . . . you will know the truth, and the truth will make you free" (John 8:31-32).

A skeptic might call this brainwashing. If you mean brainwashing is washing truth from the brain, of course not. If you mean dealing as ruthlessly as possible with anything that compromises thinking accurately about life, then yes, this is brainwashing at its very best. Consider some examples:

Athletic competition: in the heat of the contest, tempers flare like match heads. Why? Invariably you're demanding something, your mind is ruled by "musts": I must win! I must perform well! I must not look bad! I must prove something!

A tight budget: you go to the mall for a stroll, and window-shopping turns to browsing, which turns to gazing, which turns to purchasing something you cannot afford. What were you thinking? You stopped thinking! Your emotions ruled you. You were justifying, sentimentalizing, lamenting. The result? Self-pity rushed in where walls of fiscal prudence fell down. You weren't ruled by the best goal.

Feeling lonely and unappreciated: this is the time you are most vulnerable to sensual indulgence such as food, drink, sleep, or sexual fantasy. Why? You give in because at that moment you believe the pleasure offered by that indulgence is best for your soul. Where's your mind?

Paul says to set your mind on things above, not on the flesh (Col. 3:1-4) but on things that are true and right and good and lovely (Phil. 4:8). But aren't things above really hard to handle? Yes! Therefore, at the point of temptation, the question is, Will you be controlled by what you see or by what you know? Faith walks by truth. Theologian D. M. Lloyd-Jones said, "Faith is thinking." The Puritans called sin an infection of the mind. You lose control when the pictures you make in your mind are skewed or distorted, or the benefits of sin look attractive and the consequences of sin are blurred and distant. In effect, Satan has shown you the bait but hidden the hook.

You feel fearful: Circumstances are dark clouds of dread and calamity, illness, or the wrath of another person. At this point fortify the mind by making the truth vivid. Preach the Word of God to yourself until you see clearly, "The Lord is my helper, whom shall I fear?" John Knox, the sixteenth-century Scottish Reformer, said, "Why should I be afraid of an earthly monarch when I was before Almighty God this morning?!" What was the result of making the truth vivid? He controlled his fears.

Other examples abound: You find yourself controlled by needing others' approval? You've forgotten you sit in the heavenlies in Christ right now. You find yourself weighed down by guilt, having to perform to get God's acceptance? The gospel of free acceptance isn't controlling your mind.

What is the method of self-control?

You need to do the Christian "two-step": faith and repentance.

"He who conceals his transgressions will not prosper, but he who confesses and forsakes them will find compassion" (Prov. 28:13).

Faith looks to Christ for forgiveness and grace, and keeps looking. Repentance confesses and forsakes sin, and asks for the Holy Spirit's power to crucify sinful desires and to create godly ones. The Spirit will empower you to take every thought captive to Christ.

"Let us also lay aside every encumbrance and the sin which so easily entangles us, and let us run with endurance the race that is set before us, fixing our eyes on Jesus, the author and perfecter of faith" (Heb. 12:1b-2a).

How do you know this is happening? On the one hand, your sin becomes increasingly odious to you, and on the other, the Savior is more desirable. In every instance of losing control you act like an unbeliever, because you think like an unbeliever. You think God is unable to help you. You think you're an orphan in this world. You deny that God has something better for you than self-indulgence.

Put positively, in essence, self-control embraces the grace of God—that He is resolutely for you in Christ. Healthy self-control will sense helplessness and flee to Jesus for grace. In Christ we know God gave us His best, not sparing Him but delivering Him up for us all. Jesus, at the cross, chose the best for us and the worst for Himself--what self-control! He did indeed pray, "Let this cup pass from Me; yet not as I will, but as you will" (Matt. 26:39). The happy result is that we will, by grace, live forever with God in the heavenly city, because Christ has even now surrounded us with the indestructible walls of His mercy and grace.

Pride

A man's pride will bring him low, but a humble spirit will obtain honor. (Prov. 29:23)

Abraham Lincoln said, "I am nothing; truth is everything."

What would you be like if you believed that? Would you be aggressive or humble, proud or gentle? If you believed you were nothing—compared with the truth--would you be prickly and unapproachable, egotistical, self-aggrandizing, nervous around others, posturing to be esteemed, vying and dying for their approval; or would you be selflessly concerned for what is right, just, true, and most edifying to everyone? Wouldn't you cherish being proved wrong if it meant knowing or promoting the truth?

Why are these questions as important as they are irritating? These questions expose us to what we otherwise hide from ourselves, namely, how self-centered we are. When what matters most is the truth--or God's glory--then you don't matter so much. When what matters most is you, then you have a problem. God calls it pride. It's a problem because God says He hates it and it will ruin you.

"The fear of the Lord is to hate evil; pride and arrogance and the evil way and the perverted mouth, I hate" (Prov. 8:13).

"A man's pride will bring him low" (Prov. 29:23).

Your pride is eating up your joy, peace, faith, and relationships.

"When pride comes, then comes dishonor, but with the humble is wisdom" (Prov. 11:2).

People either know they have pride or they don't see it. Those who are self-consciously arrogant and proud of it are in real trouble--with God. Those who see their pride, struggle with it, and want to deal with it, are the healthiest people on earth. But many people don't see their pride. Why wouldn't people see how proud they truly are? Their pride! They're too proud to admit there's a dark side to their hearts. Here are a few tests to see whether pride is working in your heart:

Questions regarding others:

How do you respond when someone tells you that you're wrong?

What do you think of a person who disrespects you?

Do you think you are better, nicer, or smarter than others?

What are you like when someone tells you what to do?

When someone criticizes you, do you wince and think, "I'm not as bad as he says"?

Do you say or do things in order to be recognized, esteemed, and valued?

How quickly do you defend yourself when accused, or lash back when criticized?

Do you make excuses when you miss an easy putt (the greens are terrible!)?

Do you need to show yourself competent, knowledgeable, and successful?

Questions regarding yourself:

What are you like when you don't get your own way?

What leads you to repent?

Are you actively seeking to change a flaw in your character, or are you pretty satisfied with the way you are?

Do you know the way your heart wears its pride?

When my oldest son was a freshman in college, he engaged a traveling evangelist who preached in an open-air forum on his campus. Because of some spurious things the evangelist claimed, my son asked him about his sin. The evangelist claimed he hadn't sinned since the day he was saved. If such self-delusion wasn't so tragic it would be comical.

Questions regarding your relationship with God:

Do you resist doing what you know God wants you to do?

When you're successful, how quick are you to thank God?

Do you praise God for gifts he has given others that are greater than yours?

Who do you really believe owns your possessions—you or God?

Do you think you are a humble person?

Are you mad at God because you think He owes you more than you have?

Proverbs is telling us that we are all born with a serious birth defect: pride. It's a major stumbling stone on the path of life. Actually, it's more like a land mine ready to blow up something. If there are a lot of blowups around you, chances are good it's because of your pride.

"Pride goes before destruction, and a haughty spirit before stumbling" (Prov. 16:18).

Pride by its nature affects our entire personalities, is tenacious and deceptive, is last to die in us, is most contradictory to reality, is likely the source from which all sins spring, and is sin for which we're not so quickly ashamed.

What is pride?

I want to express appreciation for C. S. Lewis's explanation that pride is always in relation to another person (C. S. Lewis, *Mere Christianity* [San Francisco: HarperSanFrancisco, 1952]).

> *Now what I want you to get clear is that Pride is essentially competitive—is competitive by its very nature—while the other vices are competitive only, so to speak, by accident. Pride gets no pleasure out of having something, only out of having more of it than the next man. . . . Once the element of competition is gone, pride is gone. (109-110)*

Perhaps we can push his definition of pride a bit further. I believe pride is not principally something you do; rather, it is something you are. It is a disposition, a way of thinking or living in the world. It is a heart motivation that seeks to assert and promote and protect self. It assumes a posture before God. Therefore, the essential question to expose pride is: Are you responding to God in accordance with who or what God is? Is your disposition congruent with God's nature? Let me illustrate. If you put an ice cube in a pot of boiling water, what usually happens? Does it usually melt? No, it *always* melts; it has to, because the fixed reaction of ice to hot is melting. Pride is an ice-cold heart immersed in the hot love of God, but doesn't melt. Pride is an unnatural reaction to God, the opposite of what should happen to the heart in the presence of God. Since his loving-kindness fills the earth, and he is a consuming fire, we should melt in His presence.

146

"The wicked, in the haughtiness of his countenance, does not seek Him. All his thoughts are, 'There is no God'" (Psalm 10:4). No wonder Proverbs 16:5 says, "Everyone who is proud in heart is an abomination to the Lord." Your pride doesn't simply ignore God, but puts you in His place:

"Son of man, say to the leader of Tyre, 'Thus says the Lord God, because your heart is lifted up and you have said, 'I am a god, I sit in the seat of gods, in the heart of the seas,' yet you are a man and not God, although you make your heart like the heart of God . . . '" (Ezek. 28:2).

What is going on in the heart? There is a progression from arrogance to deception to invincibility.

Notice that progression in Obadiah 3: "The arrogance of your heart has deceived you, you who live in the clefts of the rock, in the loftiness of your dwelling place, who say in your heart, 'Who will bring me down to earth?'" We see it also in 2 Chronicles 26:16: "But when [Uzziah] became strong, his heart was so proud that he acted corruptly, and he was unfaithful to the Lord his God, for he entered the temple of the Lord to burn incense on the altar of incense." (This was an act reserved only for priests.) See the progression: By the Lord's help he became strong (it is always that way; we owe it all to God). Because he became strong, he thinks he is something (his heart was proud), and acts above the law, according to his own rules. Pride traffics in this dynamic: right facts, wrong conclusion. He said, I am powerful (a fact); therefore, I am something (wrong conclusion). He should have said, I am powerful (a fact); therefore, I am blessed and responsible to give God the glory and to seek Him all the more in humble, grateful dependence (right conclusion). We're all like turtles on a fencepost--someone else put us there. C. H. Spurgeon said, "When you have your best suit on, remember who paid for it."

Howard E. Butt, longtime chairman of the H-E-B grocery chain from Texas, which did a measly $11 billion in business in 2003, said in an article titled, "The Art of Being a Big Shot":

It is my pride that makes me independent of God. It's appealing to me to feel that I am master of my fate, that I run my own life, call my own shots, go it alone. But that feeling is my basic dishonesty. I can't go it alone. I have to have help from other people, and I can't ultimately rely on myself. I'm dependent on God for my next breath. It is dishonest of me to pretend that I'm anything but a man—small, weak, and limited. So, living independent of God is self-delusion. It is not just a matter of pride being an unfortunate little trait and humility being an attractive little virtue; it's my inner psychological integrity that's at stake. When I am conceited, I am lying to myself about what I am. When I am pretending to be God and not man my pride is the idolatrous worship of myself. And that is the national religion of hell.

Why do we have it?

Pride is in our nature because our nature changed at the fall. The heart of Satan's deception to Adam and Eve was essentially, "You are a competent judge of truth independent of God. Decide for yourself. Only you can determine what will make you happy. You have the right to autonomously weigh God's Word versus mine versus your opinions." On the contrary, God says, trust the expert. We do that in all walks of life—with doctors, car mechanics, investors, you name it. So why shouldn't we trust the expert with the nature of created life? God created it and He's the expert. Satan would say, "Don't be so sure." Do you see that as the height of arrogance? Do you see why pride is a huge lie? We don't ultimately know anything truly apart from God. Nothing in the universe has its meaning apart from, or independent of, God. If you want to live by self-rule for self-pleasure for self-praise, you are well motivated by pride. Can you allow your glory to be defined by someone infinitely more glorious than you? The good news is, once you've met Him, you'll want to live for His glory.

How do we overcome it?

1. Admit that the root of "surface sins" is pride. Think carefully about how pride lies beneath so many of your struggles. How are self-concern and self-promotion motivating you?

Lying: I'll look bad if the truth be known.

Greed: I deserve this.

Lust: I'm worthy of pleasure.

Gossip: I'm important because I know secrets.

Anger: How dare you do that to me!

Judgmental: I'm always right.

Laziness: I have a right to use time as I see fit.

Lawlessness: I'm an exception to the rule.

Cheating: I'm a special case.

Shyness: I'm unwilling to be known.

Unapologetic: I don't fail or make mistakes.

Pretentiousness: My reputation is paramount.

Boasting: I need to be recognized.

Unapproachable: I'm too important for you.

When the first person singular pronouns (I and me) drive your thinking, it's usually because of pride.

2. Look beneath the civil surface of niceness that we all put on and discover attitudes toward others that pride produces: you focus on their failures, being critical and fault-finding; you look down on them with little compassion; you are quick to excuse yourself and to shift blame to others; you protect your image or reputation; you get defensive when criticized; it is hard to admit being wrong; you are driven to be recognized; you are controlling or inflexible (it's my way or the highway); you are unteachable— you know it all already.

All of this ultimately falls under the category of Proverbs 25:27:

"It is not good to eat much honey, nor is it glory to search out one's own glory." Honey, like finding out how wonderful you are, is sweet to the taste but only in small doses. To dwell on one's own glory is as sickening as too much honey. What is the only way out of slavery to one's own glory?

3. Seek out the glory of the most humble person in the world.

You need to fall in love with someone who is both so great that he will humble you and so humble that he will melt away your self-glory. Mere humans will only provoke your pride because they, too, are prideful. Where do you meet a person who is humble without any sinful pride? Where do you meet a person who, though flawless, doesn't provoke you to envy? In Matthew 11:28 Jesus tells us that He is that humble man: "Come to Me, all who are weary and heavy–laden, and I will give you rest. Take My yoke upon you and learn from Me, for I am gentle and humble in heart, and you will find rest for your souls."

You will never find true humility until you experience the humble and gentle heart of Jesus. What irony! Only the sinless

Jesus could claim to be humble without doing so in pride. We discover His heart not in our strength or in our doing for the Lord, but in our brokenness and in our desperation over our sin. David relates his trauma of debilitating sin in Psalm 38:3-7:

> *There is no soundness in my flesh because of Your indignation; there is no health in my bones because of my sin.*

> *For my iniquities are gone over my head; as a heavy burden they weigh too much for me.*

> *My wounds grow foul and fester because of my folly. I am bent over and greatly bowed down; I go mourning all day long.*

> *For my loins are filled with burning, and there is no soundness in my flesh.*

Sin is wearying, but so is self-consumption. Pride makes you restless, needing to prove yourself; but when have you proven yourself for certain? Isn't there always more to do? Isn't there always someone ahead of you, better than you? Pride wears us out, trying to do the impossible--always defending ourselves from criticism. Who are we kidding? What a burden to bear, hiding from others the truth we know about ourselves. When you trust Jesus for your salvation, He humbly pays the death penalty at the cross that your pride deserves. Jesus in His gospel says, "You are evil, you crucified Me, but I'll forgive you and clothe you in My righteousness so that My Father will love you the way He loves Me." The gospel answers pride in that while pride wants me to look good, the gospel actually makes me good. In Christ I am already as righteous in God's sight as I'll ever be. Now I have nothing to prove to God, and consequently, to anyone else. That's why Paul says we boast not in ourselves but in Christ; everything that makes us good is from Him! "But by the grace of God I am what I am . . . " (1 Cor. 15:10).

The gospel frees you to say, "I am nothing and God is everything," but, paradoxically, once you say that you become something: the very sons and daughters of God, the apple of His eye, His precious treasure, a vessel to hold His life, a trophy of His grace. He gently fights against your pride for your welfare and rest. What is the evidence of that? Your pride begins to melt; you realize you can in fact swallow it and not choke to death. He begins to break you of your self-reliance. You'll want to be forgiven. You'll want cleansing like never before. You'll see that Jesus gives a dignity you could never earn--the status of a son of God.

* * * * * * * * * *

You are the love of all my life

You are the living spring

You are the joy that finds my heart

Giver of all good things

What am I without you; what am I without you?

You are the day that rules the night

You are the hope in me

All that I have descends from you

All I could ever be

What am I but a piece of earth

Breathing holy breath

What am I but a wayward child

Given life for certain death

Pride

You are the everlasting king

You are the risen lord

That you would come and fill my soul

This is beyond a dream

What am I without you; what am I without you?

(Twila Paris)

Humility

A man's pride will bring him low,
But a humble spirit will obtain honor. (Prov. 29:23)

Did you hear the story about the minister, the Boy Scout, and the computer expert flying as the only passengers on a small plane? The pilot came back to the cabin and said that the plane was going down, but there were only three parachutes for four people. The pilot added, "I should have one of the parachutes because I have a wife and three small children." So he took one and jumped. The computer whiz said, "I should have one of the parachutes because I am the smartest man in the world and everyone needs me." So he took one and jumped. The minister turned to the Boy Scout, and with a warm smile said, "You are young and I have lived a rich life, so you take the remaining parachute, and I'll go down with the plane." The Boy Scout said, "Relax, reverend, the smartest man in the world just picked up my knapsack and jumped out!"

Now I like that story, not because it makes the minister look good, but because it illustrates so well the scripture before us, which fleshes out the relationship between pride and humility. Like the brilliance of the stars seen only in contrast with the darkness of the night, so the beauty of humility is seen in contrast with the darkness of pride. We see humility and pride in relief as we analyze the story in terms of motivation, action, and result. The computer expert, in pride, is motivated by self-importance: I deserve this! The minister, in humility, is motivated by gratitude: I have lived a rich life. The pride of the computer expert compels him to action: he steals from others to take for himself. The humility of the minister leads him to action: deferring to another for the other's welfare. The result of pride is the desired opposite: instead of self-preservation it produces self-destruction. The result of humility is the honor, not sought, of deliverance from danger. Just as the story works for its irony--the smartest man in the world can't tell the difference between a knapsack and a parachute--so pride and humility are understood in terms of irony. Let's explore four points of irony.

1. Humility, the virtue that proves us most genuine, can easily be counterfeited.

a. You can be humbled without being humble.

If you make a mistake and blame others, you haven't been humble. Affliction may bring you low in countenance or posture but your heart may remain proud--I don't deserve this! But do you really know what you deserve? Humble people do.

b. You can evidence humble behavior outwardly without inwardly being humble.

Absalom's conduct at the gates of Jerusalem in 2 Samuel 15:5 illustrates a man using false humility to gain power over others.

c. You can behave religiously and still be proud.

Jesus saw many religious people in His day who prayed and gave great gifts to the church, but condemned them as proud and wanting to be noticed by people.

d. You can think less of yourself and still not be humble.

Sometimes when people think less of themselves it is because of a prideful desire to be better than they are. Pride is self-absorption, self as greatest concern, and you may compare yourself with others and feel like a worm because you aren't as talented as they are (self-pity). Humility isn't thinking less of yourself; it is thinking of yourself less. Does God say you are worthless? No, you're a creature made in His image with incalculable worth, despite your sin. Yes, our sin makes us wicked and unworthy, but not worthless.

2. The things that tempt us to pride should make us humble.

All of us have things we think make us good or worthy. These things answer the question, Why should others be impressed with me?

Wealth: "By your great wisdom, by your trade you have increased your riches, and your heart is lifted up because of your riches . . . " (Ezek. 28:5). "Instruct those who are rich in this present world not to be conceited . . . "(1 Tim. 6:17).

Beauty: "Your [the prince of Tyre] heart was lifted up because of your beauty . . . " (Ez. 28:17). "Charm is deceitful and beauty is vain, but a woman who fears the Lord, she shall be praised" (Prov. 31:30).

Status: "But when his heart was lifted up and his spirit became so proud that he [the king of Babylon] behaved arrogantly, he was deposed from his royal throne, and his glory was taken away from him" (Dan. 5:20).

Success: "You [Amaziah] have indeed defeated Edom, and your heart has become proud" (2 Kings 14:10).

Popularity: "Woe to you when all men speak well of you . . . " (Luke 6:26). "They loved the approval of men rather than the approval of God" (John 12:43).

Why can't we derive our worth from these?

a. You can't derive worth from what's borrowed. All that we have is on loan as a stewardship from God. If I borrow your expensive car, I can't claim that I'm somehow wealthier by driving your car. That's pride: I want to look good regardless of whether or not I am good. Simon the magician wanted to look good and Peter said his heart was full of iniquity (Acts 8:18-24).

b. Each of these can be taken away; they're on a string. Nebuchadnezzar starkly illustrates this. God removed him from being king of Babylon "and he was driven away from mankind and began eating grass like cattle . . . " (Dan. 4:33).

c. Each is a gift of God requiring great responsibility to use for God's glory. What counts ultimately is the glory God gets from your life. The famous architect Frank Lloyd Wright said, "Early in life I had to choose between honest arrogance and hypocritical humility. I chose the former and have seen no reason to change." I wonder if anyone explained to him a third option: honest humility?

d. Each gift should evoke bewilderment: why should someone like me be given so much? That's what humility thinks. Humility freely acknowledges that my graces make God look good.

e. These things make you look good before others but can't make you good before God. What qualifies you for heaven is not talent--however you measure it--but sinless holiness. "Riches do not profit in the day of wrath" (Prov. 11:4). If you want the applause of men, you have it--but that's all (Matt. 6:5). "If I have . . . all knowledge . . . but do not have love, I am nothing" (1 Cor. 13:2).

3. Pride never finds the thing it seeks.

"A man's pride will bring him low, a the humble spirit will obtain honor" (Prov. 29:23). What is pride seeking? Honor, recognition, esteem, avoiding being low. There is such a thing as honor among men, and God says it's temporary and fleeting, and that only He gets it right. "That which is highly esteemed among men is detestable in the sight of God" (Luke 16:15).

By definition, honor has to be given and can't be taken. Like the "most popular" award in high school, you don't award yourself. By its nature popularity is determined by the populace. You are popular only if others say so. The same is true with honor. "Let another praise you, and not your own mouth" (Prov. 27:2). A wide receiver in the NFL wore a jacket on the sidelines with writing on the back claiming, "Hall of fame 20??." Clearly, that is not for him to decide, but for the objective observers of his performance. A 2009 inductee into the baseball Hall of Fame, Ricky Henderson, described himself as "the greatest ever." Again, that is for others to decide, not him.

You are honored not because you say so, but because others determine it so. God says, I'm the only one in the world who can give ultimate honor because I know all things and I understand people's motives. Hence, "Humble yourselves under the mighty hand of God, that He may exalt you at the proper time" (1 Peter 5:6). Your job is to stay under the mighty hand of God and let Him direct and use you as He desires, while God's job is to exalt you at the time of His choosing. Do you see? When you insist on self-glory, you lose it. Where do you find it? In the truth.

The foundation of human greatness is truth. Humility is the fruit of accurate self-knowledge. You see yourself as you are. You have to use a measuring standard outside yourself. Our tendency is to cut ourselves slack. "Every man's way is right in his own eyes" (Prov. 21:2).

My fun story about humility concerns our Labrador retriever. When my wife took her to the veterinarian for her first checkup, the vet glowed with compliments for our dog. Among other things, she said, "This dog is very intelligent and highly motivated by food." When I heard that I said to my wife, "Sounds like our Lab is a walking picture of our marriage. You are highly intelligent and I am highly motivated by food!"

Seriously, if you asked the average man on the street, he would say, "Yes, I am a basically a good, decent person." That is because he typically compares himself with Hitler, and naturally will come out smelling like a rose. But when you use God's standard of moral perfection as delineated in His law, we all fall short. "All have sinned and fall short of the glory of God" (Rom. 3:23).

Therefore, humility says, I'm to blame. I'm not what I was made to be, and it's no one's fault but mine. My sin keeps me from godliness; I seek my glory not God's. Humility says, I don't know about your heart, but it can't be as bad as mine. Pride says, I'll study your infirmities and my excellencies. Humility says, I'll study my infirmities and your excellencies. How in the world do you get to that point?

4. The way to honor is to admit your poverty.

"When pride comes, then comes dishonor, but with the humble is wisdom" (Prov. 11:2). The word for pride suggests a boiling up; the proud, like boiling water, in effect say, Don't touch me or you'll get hurt. But, "when pride comes, then comes dishonor" as an unwelcome guest (Waltke, *Proverbs*, Ch. 1-15, 483), which is the last thing the proud want--to be dishonored.

The word for humility is also used for a pipe or water conduit, implying that the humble person understands that we merely possess good things as unworthy vessels. "Before destruction the heart of man is haughty, but humility goes before honor" (Prov. 18:12). The word for humility here means "of low eyes," or "to stoop down." Pride looks down on others, humility looks up.

Who can do this? Our natural hearts can produce only pride. Jesus said, "A good tree cannot produce bad fruit, nor can a bad tree produce good fruit" (Matt. 7:18). Attempting more good works, trying harder, cleaning up your act, going to church more frequently, all that is like spraying water on a bad tree, or polishing rotten fruit. That won't change its nature and may only make it produce more badness because the problem is systemic. You need a new heart. Here's the irony: to work right as a human being, you have to confess you don't work right. The great promise of the Bible is that God does the impossible. He does for us what we can't do for ourselves; He gives a new heart.

"Yet to this day God has not given you a heart to know, nor eyes to see, nor ears to hear" (Deut. 29:4).

"The Lord your God will circumcise your heart and the heart of your descendants, to love the Lord your God with all your heart and with all your soul, so that you may live" (Deut. 30:6).

"I will sprinkle clean water on you, and you will be clean; I will cleanse you from all your filthiness and from all your idols. Moreover, I will give you a new heart and put a new spirit within you; and I will remove the heart of stone from your flesh and give you a heart of flesh. I will put My Spirit within you and cause you to walk in My statutes, and you will be careful to observe my ordinances" (Ezek. 36:25-27).

"Therefore, if anyone is in Christ, he is a new creature; the old things passed away; behold, new things have come" (2 Cor. 5:17).

How do you recognize a new heart in operation? A new heart is always discovering, ironically, old facts: the holiness of God, the sinfulness of sin, and the love of Christ. When you stop viewing yourself through the magnifying glass of self-appreciation (in which you invariably appear in your own eyes better than you are), and start viewing yourself through the magnifying glass of Christ's love, you'll want to say with humble John the Baptist, "He must increase, but I must decrease" (John 3:30).

Here is a test of true humility. Can you honestly pray this prayer, a wonderful song by John Berridge?

Jesus, cast a look on me,

Give me sweet simplicity,

Make me poor and keep me low,

Seeking only Thee to know.

All that feeds my busy pride

Cast it evermore aside,

Bid my will to Thine submit,

Lay me humbly at Thy feet.

Do you really want to be low? Are you willing to dispense with all that feeds your pride? Is it your fervent prayer to be laid humbly at Jesus' feet?

As you grow with a new heart, the Spirit will show you the holiness of God, and, correspondingly, He'll uncover your sin. Repent of your sin and look in faith to Christ, trusting that His cross is all-sufficient for your forgiveness. When you do this you won't be proud of what you are, but humble for what you lack. You'll think, considering all the grace that's mine, I should be much better than I am, and should have accomplished much more for God than I have.

You will rest increasingly in the love of Christ for you. You will desire Jesus to get the credit, rather than take it yourself. You will be content to be laid aside if God chooses to use other tools. You'll be willing to take reproof for sin, rather than hide behind self-righteousness. Reproof to the proud is gasoline on a fire; reproof to the humble is cold water in the desert. You will be able to bear the reproach of your enemies, knowing that you were God's when He saved you. You will stop complaining that you have so little, and start wondering why you have so much. The worst piece God carves is better than you deserve.

Do you see the irony? You become rich by admitting your poverty.

Pride can be killed, but not by its owner. Only Jesus Christ can subdue your proud heart. He does so by bringing you to His cross.

There we see the ultimate irony: a gruesome criminal's death brings forth glorious eternal life. The Prince of Peace went to war against your sins. The only truly holy man to ever live became filthy sin on the cross. Jesus took all His power and used it to become weak. The God who blesses became a curse on a tree He Himself had made. Jesus takes your sin and exchanges it for His righteousness. You can give Him your pride, and He'll honor you in exchange: Jesus says, Sit at My table with Me. The richest, most blessed, most secure, most peaceful and joyful people . . . have nothing to brag about.

That is the irony of grace. Jesus' good news, the light of the gospel, burns away the fog of our self-importance, and then we see how precious we are to God, that His Son would die for us. Oh the irony! The humble heart is God's palace.

For great is the glory of the Lord. For though the Lord is exalted, yet He regards the lowly; but the haughty He knows from afar. (Ps.138:5b-6)

Do nothing from selfishness or empty conceit, but with humility of mind regard one another as more important than yourselves; do not merely look out for your own personal interests, but also for the interests of others. Have this attitude in yourselves which was also in Christ Jesus, who, although He existed in the form of God, did not regard equality with God a thing to be grasped, but emptied Himself, taking the form of a bond-servant, and being made in the likeness of men. Being found in appearance as a man, He humbled Himself by becoming obedient to the point of death, even death on a cross. For this reason also, God highly exalted Him, and bestowed on Him the name which is above every name, so that at the name of Jesus EVERY KNEE WILL BOW, of those who are in heaven and on earth and under the earth, and that every tongue will confess that Jesus Christ is Lord, to the glory of God the Father. (Paul's hymn to humility, Phil. 2:3-11)

Case Study on Social Pride

Do not claim honor in the presence of the king,
and do not stand in the place of great men;
for it is better that it be said to you, "Come up here,"
than for you to be placed lower in the presence of the prince,
whom your eyes have seen. (Proverbs 25:6-7)

It's usually not hard to spot self-promotion. Unmistakable are the words and body gestures that say, "Look at me, aren't I something!" It runs rampant in the sports arena in our world. In Luke 14:7-15, Jesus notices a case of self-promotion at a dinner party at the house of a prominent Pharisee. He comments on it to some of the guests, using a parable drawn right from Proverbs 25:6-7.

And he began speaking a parable to the invited guests when he noticed how they had been picking out the places of honor at the table, saying to them, "When you are invited by someone to a wedding feast, do not take the place of honor, for someone more distinguished than you may have been invited by him, and he who invited you both will come and say to you, 'Give your place to this man,' and then in disgrace you proceed to occupy the last place.

"But when you are invited, go and recline at the last place, so that when the one who has invited you comes, he may say to you, 'Friend, move up higher'; then you will have honor in the sight of all who are at the table with you. For everyone who exalts himself will be humbled, and he who humbles himself will be exalted."

Luke explains the situation that sets up Jesus' commentary. The Pharisees were "watching him closely" to see whether He would heal a man with dropsy, on the Sabbath. He performs the miracle in order to set up the parable. Jesus heals the man to expose their foolish thinking about the kingdom of God.

The kingdom of God is coming; the King is present. But He's not bringing it the way many Jews expected their Messiah to come, in military victory. Instead, the effects of the curse are being reversed. Jesus is demonstrating the powers of the age to come, the new heaven and the new earth, when all will be in perfect order.

Everywhere Jesus goes He performs the deeds of the kingdom and preaches the demands of the kingdom. The kingdom is for the weak, the lowly, the infirm, and the disenfranchised. God loves to make the poor rich. Bursting forth from Jesus are life, love, truth, healing, and these always create a reaction.

The healing also exposes the Pharisees' foolish thinking about how we enter and advance in the kingdom. Not only did the Pharisees misapply the law, but they maintained a cold-hearted approach to lowly people, the down-and-out. They held contempt for the lame, blind, and poor, thinking that they were that way because of the curse of God. In seeking to keep themselves from the lowly, they only hid from themselves the curse of their own pride and self-promotion.

Their thinking could be summed up as follows:

God helps those who help themselves. God adds strength to the strong. If you're a good person God will accept and bless you. Bad people get what they deserve.

So Jesus exposes their pride. "Hey gentlemen, I notice you took the place of honor at the table when you came in. Do you know how risky that is if you haven't seen the guest list? So here's some helpful advice for social grace."

"Do not exalt yourself in the king's presence, and do not claim a place among great men; it is better for him to say to you, "Come up here," than for him to humiliate you before a nobleman" (Luke 14:8-10, expanding Prov. 25:6-7).

Good advice? Yes. But what's the connection to the kingdom of God?

There's a problem with the kingdom: it doesn't work the way we think it should. It is in fact a countercultural revolution, the upside-down kingdom. If you and I had a kingdom, we'd prefer people who can pay their way, who can give back to us. We'd recruit people who behave themselves and are self-sufficient. But, in God's kingdom, the way in and forward is not what we'd expect. Jesus has to reveal that to the Pharisees and to us. Although there is this urge in us that insists on self-promotion, the way into the kingdom is self-humbling. The nature of the kingdom is that we do not exalt ourselves; just the opposite, we humble ourselves and exalt others. We are filled by filling others. Therefore, pride and self-absorption hinder us in the kingdom; they snuff out kingdom values.

Jesus sets out the logic of His revolutionary kingdom with this principle:

"For everyone who exalts himself will be humbled, and he who humbles himself will be exalted" (Luke 14:11).

This principle raises at least five questions:

1. What is self-exaltation?

Self-exaltation is any form of bringing attention to oneself. To exalt is to lift up or place in the center, to magnify above all other things.

For example, we do this when we pout if we don't get our way, insist on giving our viewpoint, make excuses for our failures, or make sure people know we're competent. There's a difference between self-exaltation and self-absorption. Though both are driven by pride, a self-absorbed person could be shy and retiring. A self-exalting person is more outwardly attention-seeking.

Why do we exalt ourselves? Self-promotion accomplishes something in our thinking. Everything we do, we do for a reason, to fulfill some motive. It seems we are driven by a need to lift up ourselves because we sense we are low. We apparently need to feel better about ourselves. Whether ashamed or failing or feeling unnoticed, self-exaltation puts us back where we think we belong. We see this immediately after the introduction of sin in the world. Adam is confronted by God, "Why are you hiding from Me," and Adam starts shifting blame to "the woman you gave me." When there's relational breakdown with God, everything else is affected.

All of us are born with an internal sense of our shame before God, our sense of inadequacy before God, our fear of His judgment, and this fuels the need to prove ourselves. In our heart of hearts we know we're not what God made us to be, yet we continue to insist, Yes I am, I'm not so bad, there is something good in me; here, let me prove it!

In order to feel better about ourselves, we typically do one of two things: either we put down others, or we attempt to get people to approve of us. Somehow, thinking less of others, magnifying their frailties, makes us feel better about ourselves.

Well, I'm glad I'm not like that! Or if we can get others to say nice things about us, to esteem us, then obviously we can feel better about ourselves. Thus, all of us have a deep insecurity, often hidden from ourselves, about who we are, an unresolved fear about where we stand in the universe.

2. Where does self-exaltation reveal itself?

Why is that an important question? Because Jesus' principle contains a warning and a promise; the warning is against self-exaltation, the promise is for exaltation. We inherently want exaltation because God made us His most precious possessions in all of creation. Psalm 8 says God made us "a little lower than the heavenly beings, and crowned [us] with glory and honor" (Ps. 8:5 ESV). But sin has spoiled the glory. We want it back, but we'll never get it on our own terms.

Self-exaltation reveals itself in three places:

a. In what you think you deserve.

The guests go immediately to the seats of honor at the party, evidently because they thought that's where they deserved to be, not because the host put them there. The disciples weren't immune to this, either. "[Jesus] began to question them, 'What were you discussing on the way?' But they kept silent, for on the way they had discussed with one another which of them was the greatest" (Mark 9:33-34).

Why do you think you deserve prominence or recognition? Why do you need people to honor you, like you, or esteem your knowledge, appearance, or abilities? Why do you demand respect from others? The best cure for this is to ask God what you deserve.

b. In relation with other people.

The host at the party doesn't get it. So Jesus has homework for him: throw a party for people who can't repay you (Luke 14:12). Can't do that? Why not? Must be that your motives for parties and such are self-serving. You won't get anything back if the lowly come to your party. They may steal some food while they're there and probably not write a "thank you" note. They might take advantage of you. You deserve better.

When is it easy to be self-exalting? When you compare yourself with bad people. Jesus told another parable to illustrate the folly of this (The Pharisee and the tax collector, Luke 18:9-14). We can always find someone who makes us look good. But when we use God's standard of righteousness, we have to agree with Paul that "there is none righteous, not even one, there is none who understands, there is none who seeks for God . . . there is none who does good" (Rom. 3:10-12).

c. In relation with God

Jesus brings this out in another parable (Luke 14:16-24). God invites everyone to His banquet feast, but they all have lame excuses why they can't come. Translated: people just don't have time for God or serious interest in His glory. Don't miss one of the key ideas here. God invites us to His banquet because we can't repay Him. We have no means. What do you owe God? Perfection. Any gap between that and what you are creates a debt in God's moral economy. What would it take to repay God for your sins? Sin requires death. The only way to pay is eternal punishment. But there is One who pays the debt for any who ask Him. Jesus is the way to the Father because He alone pays the price by His death on the cross. Jesus Christ cried out on the cross, *tetelestai*, a Greek commercial term meaning paid in full, the debt is erased.

3. When will the self-exalting be humbled?

There are two ways to answer this question. First, when God wants to do it. He does it; notice that "be humbled" is the passive voice. Therefore, don't worry about God humbling others. Isn't the question, When will God humble you? And the answer? The sooner the better. Second, for certain, all will be humbled at the final judgment. Positively, for believers, "I'm not getting what I deserve! I'm getting what I don't deserve!" Negatively, for unbelievers: "I blew it; I'm getting what I deserve! I have no one to blame but myself." People will see the extreme worth of God and be excruciatingly aware of what they owed Him.

4. When will the humble be exalted?

"Humble yourselves under the mighty hand of God, that he may exalt you at the proper time" (1 Peter 5:6).

Notice again that "exalt" is passive: "will be exalted." Exalt means to lift up, to honor, to prize as valuable. No one exalts himself; God does it "at the proper time." God will certainly exalt the humble at the final resurrection by granting them glorified bodies and by giving them rule over the earth. I think angels will be tempted to bow down to us. God can also exalt you any time He wants.

The point is, don't worry about it or seek it. Let God honor you. Resist promoting yourself; there's sweeter, greater joy and glory found in promoting others. Proverbs 27:2 says it well,

"Let another praise you, and not your own mouth, a stranger, and not your own lips."

171

5. How do you humble yourself?

Ask God to show you what you're like and to oppose your proud thoughts and motives (James 4:6,10). Question your motives. Why am I doing this? Is there self-promotion in my words or actions?

Admit to Him you are a vacuum of self-concern. Explore the "I deserve" mentality. What do you really deserve? Plead with the Lord to expose your failures and to change you. Seek the Lord's glory. This is the only thing that can rescue you, a passion for His glory. The Holy Spirit creates this using the Word of God and worship.

Whenever you do something for someone else, seek payment first from Christ. We don't know we have a servant's mindset until we're treated like one. If you don't mind people treating you like a servant, you're getting there. If you resent people treating you less than you think you deserve, you don't have a servant's heart.

Come before the cross. See Jesus dying because of you and for you. Think hard about the gospel. Cheer up, you're a lot worse than you know, but you're more loved than you ever dreamt possible.

Case Study on Intellectual Pride

The words of Agur the son of Jakeh, the oracle.
The man declares to Ithiel, to Ithiel and Ucal:
Surely I am more stupid than any man, and I do not have the
understanding of a man. Neither have I learned wisdom, nor
do I have the knowledge of the Holy One. Who has ascended
into heaven and descended? Who has gathered the wind in His
fists? Who has wrapped the waters in His garment? Who has
established all the ends of the earth? What is His name or His
son's name? Surely you know! Every word of God is tested;
He is a shield to those who take refuge in Him. (Prov. 30:1-5)

Since 1991 the world has enjoyed a new kind of book--the "For Dummies" series. What started with how to use a DOS computer system has grown to a series of books, 125 million in print in 39 languages, with topics ranging from dating, to Shakespeare, golf, opera, vitamins, migraines, drawing, roses, sleep disorders, Irish history, Lewis and Clark, spirituality, Christianity, and neuro-linguistic programs, to name a small sampling.

The author's premise is simple. We know you don't get this subject, but it's not as hard as you think. We're going to make it simple; we're dummying this down so that anyone can learn this. This publishing enterprise works because in our culture we place value on gaining knowledge; plus, it's permissible to admit you're a dummy with respect to certain realms, such as neuro-linguistic programming. All you need is $22 to buy the book. But what about life--your meaning and purpose? Would you feel at ease buying *Justifying Your Existence for Dummies*? That may cost $22, but it would also take a huge dose of humility to admit, I don't really know myself, how to live, why I'm here, or how to get to the afterlife.

The author of this Proverbs text, Agur, does have that humility. Think of the shoes he's filling, the act he has to follow. The wisest man in the history of the world, Solomon, has just written his magnum opus, his treatise on how life works, how the moral fiber of the world is woven, how to live long, healthy, wealthy, and wise--and he has everything right! Now Agur weighs in as a newcomer and he's painfully honest about his need for the book, *Figuring Out Life for Dummies*, or *What's It Mean to be Human for Dummies*. He's admitting he read *Why You Exist for Dummies,* for the twentieth time, and he finally gets it. He didn't know what kind of person he was, until now.

Are you as humble and so full of grace?   You can be. How? You need to answer three critical questions raised by the text.

1. How do you escape the problem of human ignorance?

Agur is saying, if you don't know everything about everything, you're potentially in danger. He discovered that the beginning of knowledge is God.

The starting point to freedom, therefore, is to admit your ignorance, to admit you don't have the answers. Your greatest strength is acknowledging your weakness. Agur's wisdom is his admission that he doesn't have it. Let's unpack that.

Agur says, "Surely I am more stupid than any man, and I do not have the understanding of a man" (Prov. 30:2). This is a confession. What gave rise to it? We can only speculate that when God graciously brought him into the covenant community he realized his pagan teachers had failed him. They taught him a worldview that didn't comport with reality. It's not that his IQ was lacking; rather, when he was taught the knowledge of the Holy One, the true God, he realized two things.

One, I was stupid, that is, in comparison with where I should be, and I don't have the understanding of a man, which means a man who knows his purpose. If there is a Creator, you have a purpose—given by the Creator. If you build a shed in the backyard for your lawn equipment, the shed doesn't rise up and proclaim that all the skunks and snakes and stray sheep in the neighborhood are going to live in here. Think again, shed, I made you for my purposes. Our lives will be filled with skunks and snakes to the extent our hearts are not controlled by our Creator. It means that if you think you are free to fashion your purpose as you might wish, or that no one can tell you what's good for you, or that you are free to define yourself by yourself, you are on a collision course with your Creator.

Is it easy to admit you don't have the answers, to admit your stupidity? No, this is actually a very difficult step for people to take. Proverbs says we are born with tenacious self-trust in our hearts. We naturally think we understand things. "Every man's way is right in his own eyes" (Prov. 21:2). "There is a way which seems right to a man, but its end is the way of death" (Prov. 14:12). Agur discovered that God made him and fashioned him in His image, and to the extent his life does not reflect the glory of God's image in knowledge, righteousness, wisdom and love, he is subhuman.

Two, he realized he had to stop fooling himself that he was a good person. "There is a kind who is pure in his own eyes, yet is not washed from his filthiness" (Prov. 30:12). Jesus said this attitude shows up in the way we criticize others. "First take the log out of your own eye, and then you will see clearly to take the speck out of your brother's eye" (Matt. 7:5). If you ride a bike through a muddy puddle, the tires throw mud up on your back. Just because you can't see it doesn't mean it's not there. Many of us look only at our "front side" where things look clean. It's even hard for religious people to admit.

175

A student in my denomination's college ministry at the University of Virginia wrote:

I came to college identifying myself as a Christian. I read the Bible, I could articulate the gospel, and I knew doctrinally where I stood on social issues that I saw as impacted by Christ. Simultaneously, I identified myself and thought of myself, like so many girls at UVA, as a good girl. I did not see a dichotomy in my self-perceived righteousness and professing Christ as savior. I was mixed up. My motives and my heart were not what my whole world believed them to be. I was not brilliant. I was not kind. I had a self-obsessed and self-glorifying heart . . .

.

2. How do you know that God alone possesses wisdom?

You ask the right questions. Many people stay far from God because their questions never move them beyond the realm of their own experiences. For some of you the questions that concern you only serve your desire for comfort and autonomous control of your circumstances. If you're basically only asking questions designed around your selfish interests, you'll never come to the knowledge of God. Let me give you an example.

I've asked many people over the years, "If you were to die tonight and stand before God and He asked you, 'Why should I let you into my heaven?' what would you say?" It's amazing how many people have answered, "I don't know, I've never thought of that." Others answer, "I'd tell God I tried to live a good life." When I ask them how good a person has to be to get into heaven, they confess they don't really know. You'd agree that if there is a heaven and a hell, then those questions are far more important than the kinds of things that preoccupy us. That people seek to avoid these questions, or deny that they will eventually die, is evident to me when I lead funeral services. I can see many of the faces in the audience simply zone out for fear of facing the inevitable.

In Proverbs 30:4 Agur poses a series of four questions that have the obvious answer: God alone.

"Who has ascended into heaven and descended?" Translated, what happens when I die? You don't know if you've never died! Is there a man who can tell you what heaven is like, how to get there safely and live to tell about it? A Bible-believing Jew knows Enoch and Elijah were taken to heaven without dying, but we've not heard from them since. If a person has gone to heaven and come back, that suggests nothing is hidden from him. Only God knows all things.

"Who has gathered the wind in his fists?" In other words, who has power and control over nature? Compared with the forces of nature, human beings know they are small, limited, frail, and dependent creatures. Have you listened closely to recordings of people fleeing catastrophic events such as tornadoes? They often are screaming, "Oh my God!" These kinds of things bring out of our hearts what is hidden deep within, our knowledge that God is the One with whom we have to do. Controlling the wind is doing the impossible, except for God.

"Who has wrapped the waters in His garment?" In the ancient world, the waters stood for chaos. Think of the churning of the ocean or a river rushing over its banks. No human being has control of the seas. What man is so large that he can bring order out of chaos? Only God.

"Who has established all the ends of the earth?" To do that you need dominion over all things, and correspondingly, authority over them. What man has dominion over all things? God alone has established the earth.

Agur asked questions with the answer: no one but God. That's why he was set free once he knew he needed revelation from God. Hence, he found the Word of God so precious. "Every word of God is tested; He is a shield to those who take refuge in Him. Do not add to His words or He will reprove you and you will be proved a liar" (Prov. 30:5-6).

3. How do you bridge the gulf between human helplessness and God's power?

Or using Proverbs 30:5, how is "[God] a shield to those who take refuge in Him?" To understand the question, we first need to ask, who needs a shield? Those being stirred mentally, those sensing two things. One, I am inept. I am limited, frail, and dependent. I am not God. Two, I am guilty. Obviously I'm not God, but I sure try to live like I am, controlling my own world as if its king, judging others, being self-sufficient, all the while failing to give the true God His reverence and due, letting Him control me. We're guilty of wanting God on our own terms.

If you don't understand this, Agur says, you're still stupid, less than human, and there's a huge disconnect in your heart. How do you know the gulf is beginning to close? First, when you believe that where you spend eternity is more important than anything in this life. Second, when you begin to experience the bigness of God. C. S. Lewis captures this in Narnia as he describes Lucy's reunion with Aslan, the Lion-King in Narnia:

"Welcome child," said Aslan. Lucy said, "Aslan, you're bigger." And he answered, "That is because you are older, little one." "Oh, not because you are?" Lucy said. "Oh, I am not. But every year you grow, you will find Me bigger."

When God gets bigger, you want to know His name. Agur concludes his questioning with, "What is His name, or His son's name?" In biblical times the name of someone was his character. Agur asks you, Do you know God simply as a concept, or personally? How do you know God personally? You know the name of His Son.

Any Hebrew reading this text would think initially of Adam, the first son of God, and of Israel, the son God called out of Egypt to be His own. But neither helps us bridge the gulf between a Holy God and our sin. Both Adam and Israel failed to be that faithful son, so God sent His eternal Son Jesus Christ from heaven as the second Adam and the true, faithful Israelite, to do for His people what they are unable to do for themselves. This is true grace: where humans fail God, God triumphs in their place.

God sent his Son because wisdom alone, as important as it is, can't save you from your sins, it can't make you perfectly righteous. Wisdom itself asks: "Who can say, 'I have cleansed my heart, I am pure from my sins?'" (Prov. 20:9). Wisdom also asks you to find the "friend who sticks closer than a brother" (Prov. 18:24).

All the questions Agur poses about God are answered in Jesus Christ.

Jesus gathered the winds in his fists when he hushed the storm on Galilee's sea. Jesus walked on the waters He controls with His own power. Jesus created the ends of the earth and has come to establish His kingdom among every people group to the ends of the earth. They are all His. He demonstrated His power and authority over molecules when he healed the sick and multiplied the loaves, and over demonic forces when he cast out demons.

But if that was the extent of it, we could call Him a miracle worker, but no more. Other religious figures have claimed to teach God's way and even to perform miracles. But which one has ascended to heaven and descended to the earth? Who can tell us what heaven is like, and be our shield to get us there safely? When Jesus rose from the dead He burst through the impossible of the universe. He secured for all who trust in Him a place in heaven forever. He actually descended from heaven at the incarnation and ascended again--perfectly competent not only to tell us what it's like, but also, because He lived perfectly in our place and died for our sins, He is unequivocally competent to usher us into heaven, unscathed by the wrath our sins deserve. He is the incarnate Word of God, shielding us from the wrath to come. In Jesus Christ the inaccessible heaven is accessible; the impossible is possible; the hidden is made known; despair turns to hope, our weariness becomes strength; God descended to become man, the innocent one bears the guilt, the dead one comes to life.

One day in the future Jesus will descend again, in blazing glory, to claim His own and to judge the earth. It will be the day when all things are made known and the fame of His name will be revealed among all the nations.

Guidance

The mind of man plans his way,
but the Lord directs his steps. (Prov. 16:9)

Suppose during a worship service you hear about a great ministry trip your church is planning, such as one many have taken to Mississippi to help with Hurricane Katrina cleanup. Your first thought is, I should go. Almost immediately your next thought is, But how will I know whether it's God's will? So you begin to ask God, Show me whether I should go on this trip.

Is that a good request? Sure it is, we all want our lives to be under God's direction, not our own, because we know God has a plan for our lives and we know that true freedom and deepest joy is found under Christ's lordship, not our own. So after the worship service you mention to some of your friends that you're considering going on the trip. You receive three responses. One of them says, "You better be sure it's God's will that you go. Pray a lot, wait and see how God moves you, wait for a clear sign from the Holy Spirit. You don't ever want to be out of the will of God." Another friend says, "Great idea, if it came to mind and it's not sin, do what you want to do, follow your heart, go for it!" Yet a third friend encourages you to be wise. "Think about your family needs, the cost on you physically, and ask a whole lot of questions before you commit. A decision like this requires wisdom and that you do your homework."

So, understandably, you're confused. Like many of us, when it comes to decision-making and the will of God, we aren't sure what pleases God. In Proverbs we've been given clear counsel how to handle the many pitfalls along the way-- money, time, sloth, sleep, food, anger, pride, sex, words--and now we see that there's another potential source of stumbling:

decision-making. Effective decision-making challenges us in a variety of ways. Some folks tend to get paralyzed, others make bad decisions, others appear to be rash and reckless, others seem always to decide selfishly, others act impetuously, while still others develop a track record of wisely charting the unknowns of life.

Can Proverbs help us with this issue? Yes. In keeping with the rest of the Bible, the basic approach is straightforward. If you must have a formula, here it is:

Make plans wisely,

according to God's precepts,

checking your heart,

and trust God.

To understand this formula, we need to examine two questions that correspond to the two phrases of Prov. 16:9.

1. What is the will of God? ("The Lord directs his steps.")

Theologians distinguish between three senses of the will of God:

a. His preceptive will

The precepts of God are His commands, His law, His statutes, the things He says He wants you to do. Where do we find this? In the Bible. Jesus summed up the will of God like this: love God with your whole heart and your neighbor as yourself. So when you woke up this morning and wondered what God wanted you to do today, you already have the answer: love Him and others. That's the will of God, the prescribed precepts of God. You can never hurt yourself obeying God. You can never enjoy godly happiness disobeying God.

Psalm 119 is a long, breathtaking meditation on the preceptive will of God, His Word.

The apostle Paul gives two examples of the preceptive will of God in 1 Thessalonians:

"For this is the will of God, your sanctification . . . " (1 Thess. 4:3).

In other words, grow in grace and perfect holiness in the fear of the Lord. Keep yourself unstained by the corruption of the world. By the Spirit subdue sin and produce the fruits of righteousness and faith.

"Rejoice always; pray without ceasing; in everything give thanks; for this is God's will for you in Christ Jesus" (1 Thess. 5:16-18). This is one way the Lord directs our steps; He shows us the way to walk safely in holiness. Therefore, when you are consciously prayerful, moving through the day in an ongoing conversation with God, especially offering thanks and seeking reasons to rejoice, you're in the will of God.

b. His desiderative will

By this, theologians mean those things God says he desires, but nonetheless does not bring to pass. Concerning you, did God desire that you obey him yesterday when you didn't? Of course He desired it. But that God allowed you to disobey Him means He permits things in which He takes no pleasure. Ezekiel 33:11 says that God "[takes] no pleasure in the death of the wicked." First Timothy 2:4 says God "desires all men to be saved and to come to the knowledge of the truth." Jesus wept over apostate Jerusalem, desiring that she repent and turn to Him. Could God have brought that about? Of course. No mere human is stronger than God. Whose fault is it that they didn't repent? Theirs, of course. God never creates sin in anyone's heart. But notice that while God desires all men to repent, He obviously hasn't decreed that such happen, or it most certainly would. This brings us to the next aspect of God's will.

c. His decretive will

By the decrees of God we understand those things God determined before time would come to pass. He is the Lord of history. He sees the beginning from the end. Whatever God decrees is unchanging and cannot be thwarted. These things can't be known by us ahead of time, except in those instances that God foretells by His prophets.

Can we know God's will looking backward? Naturally, whatever happens is God's will. Was Hurricane Katrina God's will? Of course it was, or many Scriptures we're examining are lies.

This is the doctrine of providence. Providence comes from the Latin pro (before) and video (to see), meaning literally, to see beforehand. Providence is God's governance of His world, by his absolute sovereignty, to accomplish his plans and purposes in the affairs of humanity, because he is King:

"God reigns over the nations, God sits on His holy throne" (Ps. 47:8; cf. 96:10).

"Our God is in the heavens; he does whatever he pleases" (Ps. 115:3).

"The counsel of the Lord stands forever" (Ps. 33:11).

"His sovereignty rules over all" (Ps. 103:19).

"For the Lord of hosts has planned, and who can frustrate it?" (Isa. 14:27).

"All the inhabitants of the earth are accounted as nothing, but he does according to His will in the host of heaven and among the inhabitants of earth; and no one can ward off his hand or say to him, 'What have You done?'" (Daniel 4:35).

"The vision is yet for the appointed time; it hastens toward the goal and it will not fail" (Hab. 2:3).

"My purpose will be established, and I will accomplish all my good pleasure" (Isa. 46:10).

"His mercies are over all his works" (Ps. 145:9).

But it's also personal:

"He performs what is appointed for me" (Job 23:14).

"In your book were all written the days that were ordained for me, when as yet there was not one of them" (Ps. 139:16).

"The Lord will accomplish what concerns me" (Ps. 138:8).

"In Him also we have obtained an inheritance, having been predestined according to His purpose who works all things after the counsel of His will . . . " (Eph. 1:10-11).

"For it is God who is at work in you, both to will and to work for His good pleasure" (Phil. 2:13).

God sees ahead of time every detail of your life, and arranges all circumstances for your good and His glory. It's like the way I used to walk on the beach with my children when they were little tikes. It was a big, big deal finding sand dollars. I'd lead them by the hand along the water's edge where sand dollars normally appear. Because of my height I could see ahead of them, and if I saw a sand dollar, I would lead the children to it, so they would have the thrill of finding it themselves. The wise person embraces providence.

How can God govern providentially? We need only to read in Proverbs absolute declarations of His kingship:

God made everything:

"The poor man and the oppressor have this in common: the Lord gives light to the eyes of both" (Prov. 29:13).

"The Lord has made everything for its own purpose, even the wicked for the day of evil" (Prov. 16:4).

God sees everything:

"The eyes of the Lord are in every place, watching the evil and the good" (Prov. 15:3).

God knows everything:

"The eyes of the Lord preserve knowledge, but He overthrows the words of the treacherous man" (Prov. 22:12).

God directs everything:

"Man's steps are ordained by the Lord, how then can man understand his way?" (Prov. 20:24).

"The king's heart is like channels of water in the hand of the Lord; he turns it wherever he wishes" (Prov. 21:1).

"The lot is cast into the lap, but its every decision is from the Lord" (Prov. 16:33).

"The horse is prepared for the day of battle, but victory belongs to the Lord" (Prov. 21:31).

God is thwarted by nothing:

"Many plans are in a man's heart, but the counsel of the Lord will stand" (Prov. 19:21).

"There is no wisdom and no understanding and no counsel against the Lord" (Prov. 21:30).

The Bible clearly tells us that God's activity must reflect His character. Therefore, His providence is perfect and good, redounds to His glory, is all comprehensive, and often mysterious. We don't always know what He is up to. "The secret things belong to the Lord our God, but the things revealed belong to us and to our sons forever" (Deut. 29:29). Waltke points out that in the first nine chapters of Genesis alone we see this irony: Abel trusted God and died; Enoch trusted God and never died; and Noah trusted God and everyone else died.

For ages, Christians have sung hymns reflecting God's sovereign purposes:

God moves in a mysterious way, his wonders to perform

He plants his footsteps in the sea, and rides upon the storm

Deep in unfathomable mines of never-failing skill,

He treasures up his bright designs and works his sovereign will

—William Cowper

Whate'er My God ordains is right, holy his will abideth,

I will be still whate'er he does, and follow where he guideth.

He is my God, though dark my road.

He holds me that I shall not fall, wherefore to him I leave it all.

—Samuel Rodigast

One thing hard to understand is how God can be absolutely sovereign, yet the choices of human beings are free and significant. We are free moral agents, given by God the liberty to choose. Yet, we can only choose according to our nature. The Bible affirms both without negating or diminishing either, so we accept it. Notice how Peter's speeches in Acts affirm both:

"This man [Jesus], delivered over by the predetermined plan and foreknowledge of God, you nailed to a cross by the hands of godless men and put Him to death" (Acts 2:23).

"For truly in this city there were gathered together against Your holy servant Jesus . . . to do whatever Your hand and Your purpose predestined to occur" (Acts 4:27-28).

Therefore, how does God govern all the acts of His creatures? In His acts of providence that we can variously label:

Uncommon: In His miracles He temporarily suspends the natural laws by which He orders the universe.

Common: He sends the rain.

188

Great: He parted the waters of the Red Sea.

Small: He provided a parking space when you most needed it.

Smiling: You get bumped from coach to business class on a long flight.

Frowning: A dear friend contracts a serious illness.

Disciplining: God chastises you for sin (Heb.12).

God does not ask us to read his providences looking forward. They are only understood like Hebrew sentences, read backward.

God asks us to trust that even when we are sinned against, God is working providentially. Joseph is a classic example. When he confronted his brothers in Egypt with their sin of leaving him for dead, he said, "You meant evil against me, but God meant it for good . . . " (Gen. 50:20).

This comforting truth is restated by Paul in Romans 8:28:

"And we know that God causes all things to work together for good to those who love God, to those who are called according to His purpose."

2. How does God guide His children? ("The mind of man plans his way.")

Now we're ready for the million-dollar question, What

189

does it mean to find God's will? Aside from God working His providential acts in our circumstances, how do we make specific choices in perplexing situations according to the will of God?

The first thing we have to affirm is that this is indeed what we want. Who among us would rather be cut loose from living in God's plan? Certainly not if it means we come under the dominion of the evil one.

Most of us think of God's will as something hidden, needing to be discovered, and usually by some manner of supernatural means. That is how pagans think about it, and you could read in books the various ways it was attempted, ranging from casting lots, to reading signs in livers (hepatoscopy), tossing arrows (rhabdomancy), praying to idols, astrology, using water to tell fortunes (hydromancy), consulting spirits, etc. (see Bruce Waltke, *Finding the Will of God: A Pagan Notion?* [Grand Rapids: Eerdmans, 1995), ch. 2]). Practices of sorcery and divination are forbidden by God in Leviticus 19:26, 31 and Deuteronomy 18:10-12.

Nevertheless, many Christians think it is spiritual to look for signs as a way to divine God's will in specific circumstances. They ask God for a sign to confirm that they should marry this person, move to this city, take this new job, etc. The testimony of the New Testament is that this is not the way to find God's will. In fact, the idea of finding God's will is foreign to the NT:

"The New Testament gives no clear command to 'find God's will,' nor can you find any particular instructions on how to go about finding God's will. There isn't a magic formula offered Christians that will open some mysterious door of wonder, allowing us to get a glimpse of the mind of the Almighty" (Waltke, *Finding the Will of God,* 12) .

The thrust of the issue is guidance. God guides us; we know that because He loves us. He has a plan for our lives, but why would He hide it from us? Therefore, if your thinking is, I'm going to do the things necessary to uncover God's will for me on this mercy trip, you're thinking about it in the wrong way. We have the Holy Spirit to help us. How does He guide us? Shall we expect Him to whisper in our ears?

Remember our verse, "The mind of man plans his way, but the Lord directs his steps" (Prov.16:9). What two things are required of you in that verse? Plan and trust his providence. So, back to my formula:

Make plans wisely,

according to God's precepts,

checking your heart,

trusting God.

First, make plans wisely.

Look at your circumstances. If you had to sit for a huge test, such as the bar exam, the day after you return, should you go on the trip? If you get car sick in 15-passenger vans, can you find another way there, or is this simply not the mercy opportunity for you? Make your plans, and God will superintend. That's why you wear a seatbelt. You're planning for the accident you hope you don't have. You save money for a rainy day need.

Planning is not unspiritual. Perhaps this point is made humorously in the light bulbs jokes that circulated a few years ago. How many charismatics does it take to change a light bulb? Two, one to turn it and one to rebuke the spirit of darkness. How many Episcopalians? Three, one to hold the ladder, one to turn the bulb, and one to pour the drinks. How many Methodists? Five, one to unscrew it and four to study any effects that might be offensive to others. How many

Calvinists? None, God has predestined when the light will go on. Now you see, that is a wrong application of providence. Do the work of planning. Those who believe in God's providence will go get another light bulb and screw it in, confident God is sovereign.

Bruce Waltke suggests a prayer like this:

"Lord, here is what I am planning to do. I think it is the right step. I've prayed about it, read your word, and sought wise counsel of others. I believe this is pleasing to you. So if you will, I plan to do this."

Then he adds, "Always leave room for things not working out quite the way you planned them" (Waltke, *Finding the Will of God*, 125).

Second, according to God's precepts.

Soak your heart and mind in God's Word. The Spirit will guide you. Scripture will speak. The precepts of God rule out certain courses you may be tempted to take. For example, if your spouse is being ugly to you, is that a sign you should get a divorce? It can't be because God forbids divorce for that particular reason. God holds you accountable to do what He wants you to do. Providence doesn't let you off the hook, as if you can say, well, if God has ordained it already, it doesn't matter what I do. That's called fatalism, and that's patently contrary to biblical thinking.

Third, checking your heart.

God works through our desires.

"Delight yourself in the Lord; and he will give you the desires of your heart" (Ps. 37:4).

Paul had a desire to evangelize certain regions, so he went. One time the Spirit sovereignly forbade him, another time he received a vision to go to Macedonia. God is free to work extraordinarily if He chooses.

When God is in control of your life, He's in control of your desires. (Waltke) But you have to be honest with your motives.

"All the ways of a man are clean in his own sight, but the Lord weighs the motives" (Prov. 16:2).

"There is a way which seems right to a man, but its end is the way of death" (Prov. 16:25).

Look at the warnings against pride in Proverbs 16 alone:

"Everyone who is proud in heart is an abomination to the Lord" (Prov. 16:5).

"Pride goes before destruction, and a haughty spirit before stumbling" (Prov. 16:18).

Wealth can deceive us very easily, too (Prov. 16:8,16).

You need to ask the Spirit to convict you concerning which desires are from God and which are selfish. Many young men have asked me, How do I know whether it is God's will that I marry my sweetheart? I ask, Do you love her and want to marry her? And if he says yes, there's his answer.

The common idea of divining God's will is either a pagan notion that we Christians need to let go of, or a mode of administration God no longer uses. God has given us a program of guidance that involves getting to know Him through His Word and letting Him shape our characters, our hearts, and our desires. Then as we know the mind of God we can live out His will. He expects us to draw close to Him first, then allow for seeking wise counsel as confirmation, or taking our circumstances into consideration and using our own sound judgment to make a decision   (Waltke, *Finding the Will of God*, 168-69).

Finally, we start and end with explicit trust in God. We remind ourselves of the fundamental truths of belonging to Christ: Lord, you're sovereign, you love me, you saved me, and you'll guide me. Argue as Paul does in Romans 8 from the greater to the lesser. If you own $1000, then you certainly own $50. If one great truth is true, than smaller truths have to be so. "He who did not spare His own Son, but delivered Him over for us all, how will He not also with Him freely give us all things?" (Rom. 8:32). Therefore, abandon your fears, doubts, or anxieties. Instead, trust the Father who has already given you His best and could not possibly withhold anything necessary for your welfare.

Loving Your Neighbor

Do not withhold good from those to whom it is due,
When it is in your power to do it.
Do not say to your neighbor, "Go, and come back,
And tomorrow I will give it,"
When you have it with you.
Do not devise harm against your neighbor,
While he lives securely beside you.
Do not contend with a man without cause,
If he has done you no harm.
Do not envy a man of violence
And do not choose any of his ways. (Prov. 3:27-31)

One morning during my prayer time my neighbor's barking dog began to get under my skin. It's annoying, and happens far too frequently. My first thought was, I'll go launch a grenade at their house. Then I thought better of that, because I didn't have a grenade launcher, so I decided just to go kill the dog. Would my son's paintball gun do the trick? Then I thought, no, I can't do that, I recently preached on self-control, and then on anger, and now I have to write about loving your neighbor. It might not look so good. Then I remembered the truth. I owe them too much.

I owe them? Do you see yourself as a debtor to your neighbors?

Most of us think of our relationships in one of three ways. One, others owe me what I desire: peace, quiet, respect, no barking dogs, no dandelions growing all over their yard next to mine. Two, we're neutral, owing each other nothing: perhaps a little help once in a while, such as that proverbial cup of sugar, but basically we just stay out of each other's way. Three, I owe them something all the time.

Do you live as a debtor to your fellow man? Sounds a bit

radical, threatening, and uncomfortable, I know. Do you
fundamentally think, what can I give, give, and give? Our text
says that this is how wisdom frames our relationships. The
frame through which you are to see your neighbor is Proverbs
3:27: "Do not withhold good from those to whom it is due,
when it is in your power to do it." God says there is a debt you
constantly have to pay to your neighbor. "Owe nothing to
anyone except to love one another . . . " (Rom.13:8). "Let us
not lose heart in doing good, for in due time we will reap if we
do not grow weary. So then, while we have opportunity, let us
do good to all people, and especially to those who are of the
household of the faith" (Gal. 6:9-10). Do you stumble in this
responsibility? Wisdom helps us determine whether you do.
How so? It distinguishes three kinds of people you meet along
the path of life.

1. People you are likely to envy.

What is envy? You are jealous that some people have what
you desire. You want to be in their place. They have some
advantage over you in their power, choices, opportunities,
appearance, possessions, or pleasures. You think your life
would be better than it is if you were in their shoes. For me,
envy is how I feel when I'm wading along the shore of a lake,
while all the beautiful boats go speeding by, pulling water
skiers, breezing through the waves. I don't want to be stuck on
the shore; I envy the people out there in the boats.

It's worth saying before moving on that you may find
yourself envying people who are living an upright life. If you
envy them out of pride, you'll feel self-pity that you don't look
as good to others as they do. If you envy them out of humility,
with a kind of holy envy, you will desire to imitate them. Paul
says to Timothy, "Now you followed my teaching, conduct,
purpose, faith, patience, love, perseverance, persecutions, and
sufferings . . . ," presumably because Timothy found them all
very desirous (2 Tim. 3:10-11).

196

But in Proverbs the warning is to "not envy a man of violence" (Prov. 3:31), or "choose any of his ways." Maybe they appear to be successful, maybe they appear to be accountable to no one. Envy is essentially blindness. You're not seeing with spiritual eyes. Envy is a fourfold blindness:

a. You basically see yourself as a poor man, failing to see the glories of belonging to the Lord expressed in Prov. 3:32-35: God is intimate with the upright (v. 32); God blesses your house (v. 33); God gives grace to the afflicted (v. 34); You will inherit honor (v. 35).

b. You don't realize their destiny, and that they, who ultimately have nothing, should envy you, who truly have everything, if you belong to Jesus. Jesus presses this issue by asking: "For what is a man profited if he gains the whole world, and loses or forfeits himself?" (Luke 9:25).

c. When you envy people who are not evil, you've put a wall between them and you. You've defined your relationship in terms of what you want rather than what you have to offer. You rob the other person of benefiting from all that God has given you, whether it be your time, talents, wisdom, experience, or listening ear.

d. Envy is a denial of the Lord's good providence. It is a faithless response to the circumstances God has ordained for you. I vividly remember when my wife and I were first married, driving home from church and passing a beautiful, sweeping lawn that framed a lovely house, and thinking, If only I had that, I'd be truly happy.

2. People who are your enemies.

Who are they?

"Do not enter the path of the wicked and do not proceed in the way of evil men. Avoid it, do not pass by it; turn away from it and pass on. For they cannot sleep unless they do evil; and they are robbed of sleep unless they make someone stumble" (Prov. 4:14-16),

These are people who will have you follow them in a lifestyle of self-indulgence. You'll believe the big lie: God is boring and no fun, but happiness can be found on your own terms in self-fulfilling activity. I knew of a missionary in Africa who began to hang with the surfer crowd and became so assimilated into their lifestyle that he eventually abandoned the faith, his wife, and children. He abandoned his Lord and his ministry for surfing.

Proverbs 1 wastes no time getting right to the danger: "My son, if sinners entice you, do not consent. If they say, 'Come with us . . . " (Prov. 1:10-11). These would-be companions promise tons of things people seek: adventure, excitement, thrill, risk, power, treasure, wealth, belonging, and camaraderie. They invite you to invest in them, enjoy the spoils of their exploits, and be in their family.

Sin always advertises itself as something better than you already have.

Wisdom, however, sees their destiny. The end of the matter is not always in sight. He who lives by the sword dies by the sword. You reap what you sow. They ambush their own lives.

It is not always obvious where certain relationships will take you. We can be fooled. We can get caught up in the moment, swept off our feet by emotions. Therefore, we must learn the discipline of asking questions. Whose best interest do they have in mind? To whom do they answer? What is the risk-reward? (Am I jeopardizing my reputation, health, physical welfare, or money, or going to jail?) Are they motivated by invincibility? (That is, they believe it's wrong only if you get caught.)

Bad company corrupts good morals, Paul warns in 1 Corinthians 15:33, implying that, as a rule, you will be influenced for the worse by people of shady character. That's why God forbids you to be yoked in a partnership with an unbeliever, such as a business or romantic relationship (2 Cor. 6:14).

But we have a problem. Jesus says to love your enemies. What does that mean? Do what's best for them. Don't repay evil for evil. Proverbs 24:17 warns us, "Do not rejoice when your enemy falls." How could we have pity when someone we deeply dislike falls? We know that could be us. Only if we knew we deserved God's wrath, but received His pity instead, could we not gloat over our enemy.

There are essentially only two kinds of people in the world: those who know they need grace and those who don't know it. Those who don't ought to be pitied by those who do, for who would know he or she needed grace except by the very grace God sovereignly bestows?

3. People you should edify.

The text assumes an obligation God established at creation, namely, that we love each other as His image bearers. When Cain violated that and slew his brother Abel, he asked God,

199

"Am I my brother's keeper?" (Gen. 4:9) That is probably the first stupid question in the history of the world.

The law given to Israel spelled out clearly our obligations in Leviticus 19:18. "You shall love your neighbor as yourself." Proverbs 3:27 is very specific about how to do this: "Do not withhold good from those to whom it is due." The idea is, love your neighbor as if he were you. Jesus said, "Treat others the same way you want them to treat you" (Luke 6:31). If you want people to treat you with respect, honesty, fairness, help, consideration, generosity, patience, or kindness, then by all means you should be the example and the pacesetter. Teach your children this principle by asking them, if there is one donut left on the table, should you grab it for yourself, or leave it for your brother? What would you want him to do for you?

"Do not withhold" assumes you have it. You're not required to give what you don't have, but only when it's in your power. You don't have to mortgage your future, but you can always listen to someone, lend a helping hand, or pray for him.

That this is stated negatively, "do not withhold," would imply you may be tempted to hold back something that is in your power to give. Why? Perhaps selfishness--I won't have enough to satisfy me. Perhaps unbelief--if I give this I may lack what I need in the future. Or perhaps judgmentally--I don't like you, you aren't worthy of my help. If you discover a person who can't pay you back, so that there's nothing in it for you, remember that Jesus promised such folks will always be with us (John 12:8).

"Do not withhold good." For whatever reason, unlike you, they can't provide for themselves. Good is anything useful to their lives, that which will make them more gloriously human, to fully experience the grace of God. For example, depending on the situation, what someone needs may be time, help, resources, expertise, something lent, comfort, a meal, a different perspective, the truth, or the gospel.

Proverbs 3:28, which says effectively, "Do not delay," attacks the attitude, "I hope he'll forget about me or get his need met some other way, and leave me alone." Several years ago I was in a hurry coming home from the store and drove past an elderly lady whose car clearly had broken down. I ignored the need, probably rationalizing that I didn't want the ice cream to melt. I got home, was cut to the quick by my sinful, selfish neglect, and immediately retraced my steps to see whether the lady still needed help. She did, and when I offered it she said, "Oh thank you, I prayed someone would come."

Verses 29-30 warn us against unnecessary provocation, either with words or actions. Notice the qualification--"if he has done no harm to you." There are cases where others harm us and it is lawful to seek compensation or retribution. God's law provides for that as a matter of justice. These verses also bind us to scrutinize our work activities for what may be harmful to others.

When the day is over, we all want to be loved like this, yet we can't love like this. It is safer to be passive, easier to be uninvolved. We put limits on what we're willing to do for others. What could make us change? Only an experience of the limitless love of God for us in Christ. Could Jesus have put limits on His love? Of course! Look how fickle the people in Jerusalem were. On His triumphal entry they hailed Him as King, but a week later screamed out, "Crucify Him!" Instead, He went to the extreme. The least indebted person in the world paid the debt of the guilty; the blameless one becomes the shamed. Such an experience of that love will utterly transform the way you serve others. "We love, because He first loved us" (1 John 4:19).

Sleep in Heavenly Peace
Proverbs 3:23-26

Then you will walk in your way securely
And your foot will not stumble.
When you lie down, you will not be afraid;
When you lie down, your sleep will be sweet.
Do not be afraid of sudden fear
Nor of the onslaught of the wicked when it comes;
For the LORD will be your confidence
And will keep your foot from being caught.
(Prov. 3:23-26)

When God promotes His wisdom, as He does throughout the prologue of Proverbs (chapters 1-9), He promises that if you keep His wisdom, "then you will walk in your way securely and your foot will not stumble" (Prov. 3:23). Because the main image for life in Proverbs is the path, that's exactly what we would expect. Wisdom identifies the potential areas of stumbling and tells us how to avoid them. But then Solomon immediately says something we may not expect. "When you lie down, you will not be afraid; when you lie down, your sleep will be sweet" (Prov. 3:24). God cares about our sleep and makes an amazing promise concerning it. Does this appeal to you, sweet sleep? It does if you struggle with insomnia or you have frequently restless nights.

Apparently, barring a physical problem, sleep is a wisdom issue. How you rest reveals whether or not you are walking in wisdom. If you walk in God's paths, it will show up in your sleep: "The fear of the Lord leads to life, so that one may sleep satisfied, untouched by evil" (Prov. 19:23). Conversely, if you are out of sync with the way God has woven the moral fabric of His creation, like tearing a newspaper from side to side, instead of top to bottom, it will likely show up in your sleep. Thank God that's so. We spend, typically, one-third of our lives sleeping. That's if you sleep an average of eight hours a day with no naps. We better find a pleasant way to spend a third of our lives!

Is sleep an issue for you? It probably depends on your age. Children tend to sleep like babies. They don't have a care in the world, normally. And many of us are envious. At least the 70 million Americans affected as of 1992 by sleep disorders (minor issues) are, and the 40 million who have chronic sleep problems (major issues). Something is going on with our sleep, because it is estimated that sleep deprivation and sleep disorders cost Americans over $100 billion in injury, death, and property damage per year. Not to mention the recent marketing of a plethora of sleep medications.

Why is our sleep important to God?

1. Physical rest is inextricably tied to psychological health.

There is no dispute with this assertion. We get grumpy when we're tired. Fatigue impairs mental and physical performance. Brainwashing is most effective under sleep deprivation. Think how heightened emotions prevent the body from resting the way it needs to: excitement keeps people awake on Christmas Eve or the eve of their wedding days; worried parents won't sleep until their teens are home safely; fear causes tossing and turning as one waits for biopsy results from the doctor. Why is this significant? Sleep may be a helpful indicator of what's going on in your heart. Aside from the fact you may have had a nap or caffeine too late in the day, or are afflicted by a disease or a lumpy mattress, if the body won't rest maybe the heart has something to say, or God is saying something to you through the heart.

Perhaps no one understood this better than Shakespeare, as reflected in Macbeth. Because of a guilty conscience, Macbeth robbed himself of "the balm of hurt minds . . . the chief nourisher of life's feast . . . ." Shakespeare said that "sleep ministers to a mind diseased" and "knits up the raveled sleeve of care."

2. Sleep reminds us of our vulnerable state.

Do we really understand how vulnerable we are? God has ordained sleep as two daily reminders. First, the need for sleep is a daily reminder of who we are in relation to God. We are limited creatures, frail, weak, needing sleep, dependent on it for healthy functioning. This serves as a picture of our need for God, who gives us life and breath. And while we're dependent and vulnerable, God is unlimited, independent, and vulnerable to nothing. "He who keeps you will not slumber. Behold, He who keeps Israel will neither slumber nor sleep" (Ps. 121:3b-4). That's why God is trustworthy. He is sovereign, all-wise, all-powerful, all-knowing, and all-awake, never asleep at the wheel. How unlike God we are! How much we need him! How you sleep reveals whether or not you believe that.

Second, the need for sleep is a daily reminder of our spiritual needs. Sleep is a synonym for death in both the Old and New Testaments, but also a metaphor for spiritual lethargy. "The Lord has poured over you a spirit of deep sleep" (Isa. 29:10). "It is already the hour for you to awaken from sleep; for now salvation is nearer to us than when we believed" (Rom. 13:11). "Let us not sleep as others do, but let us be alert and sober" (1 Thess. 5:6). What is spiritual sleepiness? You may be too tired to care! It is to spiritual reality what sleep is to physical reality: you are oblivious to God's glory, indifferent to what He is doing in the world, and drowsy with respect to your need of forgiveness and the dangers of sin. You are in the fog as to how self-centered you really are.

What are some signs of spiritual malaise? God feels distant; your heart is cold; you have no appetite for the Word of God; you have little gratitude; you are at peace with sin; you are compassionless toward others; your worship is rote. What should you do about it? Confess this to the Lord and ask Him to change you. Confess this to close friends and have them pray for you. Pray as Paul taught you in Ephesians 1:18: "I pray that the eyes of your heart may be enlightened . . . ." We're droopy-eyed and forgetful. We need light from God.

How does God warn us about sleep?

The Bible addresses three sleep scenarios:

1. Sleeping when you should not sleep.

Perhaps the most famous illustration of this is with the disciples sleeping when Jesus agonized in prayer in the Garden of Gethsemane. At Jesus' greatest time of needing His friends, they slept. Jesus firmly rebukes them, "could you not keep watch for one hour," yet is amazingly kind: "The spirit is willing, but the flesh is weak" (Mark 13:37-38). David apparently experienced sleep deprivation because of unconfessed sin (Ps. 32:3-4). Paul warns us to resolve anger lest our sleep be affected: "Do not let the sun go down on your anger" (Eph. 4:26). Proverbs 6:1-5 exhorts us not to sleep until we remedy a wrong. Proverbs also depicts various scenarios where unfulfilled obligations should keep us from sleep. Don't sleep just because you are lazy: "Laziness casts into a deep sleep, and an idle man will suffer hunger" (Prov. 19:15). Don't sleep when there is something more important to do, such as the harvest (Prov. 10:5). There is a time for everything; wisdom knows when to work and when to rest, and at all times not to love sleep (Prov. 20:13).

2. Not sleeping when you should sleep.

The two kinds of people who fall into this category look very different, though they have same motive. On the one hand, the driven person can't stop because he thinks he's too important. Unbridled ambition breeds, "I'm invincible, it all depends on me." Psalm 127:1-2 exposes the vanity of this frantic activity: "Unless the Lord builds the house, they labor in vain who build it; unless the Lord guards the city, the watchman keeps awake in vain. It is vain for you to rise up early, to retire late, to eat the bread of painful labors; for He gives to His beloved even in his sleep."

On the other hand, the undisciplined person stays up too late, watches TV, surfs the net, or leaves too much to the last minute, when he should be sleeping. Disciplined sleep is resting in light of your priorities. Your best sleep should precede your most important activities, such as corporate worship, Bible study, or work. What are you saying about your priorities when you stay up late on the evening before worship and it means coming to church in a fog? Are you ready to give God your best? Is He worthy of your best efforts? If you were in training for an athletic contest, you'd be careful to get the rest your body needs. Corporate worship is, among other things, training for glory. It's exercise for our souls to be strong all week (Heb. 10:24-25).

Both errors are motivated by pride: I want to do what I want to do, my way. There is a glorious exception: foregoing sleep in dire ministry situations. Paul in 2 Corinthians 6:5 and 11:27 refers to sleeplessness for the sake of the gospel.

3. Sleeping when you should sleep.

Obviously, you should sleep when you need it. Undoubtedly, Jesus slept, probably in crude conditions, since the "Son of Man has nowhere to lay his head" (Matt. 8:20). Except for the last night of His life, during which I doubt He slept at all, I believe Jesus sleep pleasantly. Why?

With respect to His humanity, He walked in perfect wisdom, embodying faultlessly Proverbs 3:23. Even though He was hunted for three years by His enemies, He was not "afraid of sudden fear nor of the onslaught of the wicked when it comes" (Prov. 3:25). Why? "The Lord will be your confidence" (Prov. 3:26). Yes, Jesus is God and God has no rivals and fears no one. But Jesus' sleep was also a function of His trust in His Father. Jesus prayed to His Father, praised His father, spoke for His father, obeyed His father, and He slept confident in His Father's love and purposes. He slept, as any of us may, under the sweet gaze of His loving Father. He trusted God His Father, as evidenced by His napping in the back of the boat on the Sea of Galilee in the midst of a storm!

Therefore, we must reason from the greater to the lesser. If the God who rules all things loves me, doesn't Himself sleep, and promises in His Word to give me what I need even in my sleep, what could possibly rob me of sweet sleep? "He gives to His beloved, even in his sleep" (Ps. 127:2). Why not lie down in peace? What life circumstance is out of God's control? David experienced this:

"I lay down and slept; I awoke, for the Lord sustains me. I will not be afraid of ten thousands of people who have set themselves against me round about" (Ps. 3:5-6)

Our sleep reveals our confidence. When everything quiets down, you know what you fear or worry about. It's like the person who stands beside a loud, busy street along a construction site, and only when he steps inside a quiet building realizes the alarm is going off on his watch. All the surrounding cacophony had drowned it out. What is the watch alarm of restless sleep indicating?

a. First, you trust a false confidence. You may be thinking, I don't have any trouble going to sleep. My head hits the pillow and the day is over. I sleep like a baby. But if that's because you have the moral awareness of a baby, that's a problem. Have you considered what is motivating you? It may be a subconscious desire to avoid dealing with God and to have excessive self-trust and autonomy. Asaph, in Psalm 73:5, observes:

"I was envious of the arrogant as I saw the prosperity of the wicked. For there are no pains in their death, and their body is fat. They are not in trouble as other men, nor are they plagued like mankind."

Here are folks who seem to be troubled by little because they are unaware or in denial that they are in trouble with God. Of course I can feel good about myself if I never bring my heart before a holy God.

But you may protest, "I'm a Christian, I do the things the Lord commands. I slept well because I read the Bible, witnessed, prayed for world missions, and didn't commit my pet sin." I call that "checklist peace." Your peace of conscience is based on your performance of a spiritual checklist. This way of living raises at least two important issues. First, what is motivating you? Is it fear? Fear that God won't accept you unless you do all that? Are you trying to get God to love you more? Is it pride? Are you building a resume of righteousness so you can feel good about yourself, or so you can tell others what you did?

Second, are your best efforts ever enough? Aren't they always tainted with pride? By whose strength did you actually do any of those good things? If that's the basis of your confidence, why did Jesus have to live in your place? Shouldn't it be overwhelming gratitude that God could actually do something with you? Humility--he used me, fathom that--is the response of the Christian.

b. It may be that your sleep reveals that you distrust your true confidence. Where this teaching brings us is to seek, not Mattress Giant or Tylenol PM, but sleep in the light. Sweet sleep is ultimately only available in the light. David muses in Psalm 4:6-8:

Many are saying, "Who will show us any good?" Lift up the light of Your countenance upon us, O Lord!

You have put gladness in my heart, more than when their grain and new wine abound.

In peace I will both lie down and sleep, for You alone, O Lord, make me to dwell in safety.

How can you sleep in the light of God's countenance and not be consumed by it? Only if you sleep secure in a refuge that has cleansed your sin and made you perfect in God's sight. That is what Jesus has accomplished in the gospel for any who ask. His confidence in the Father led Him to the cross, where He purchased for every believer peace with God, and thus the full right to sleep in heavenly peace.

Why We Eat

Give us this day our daily bread. (Matt. 6:11)

Perhaps you've heard the statistic that most automobile accidents occur within 20 miles of home. I assume that's because we're tempted to let our guard down in the familiar and mundane. Proverbs says the same is true about trouble spots in life. It's not in the unusual places of life, but rather in the ordinary and mundane, along the path we take every day, that we stumble morally. The potholes are the familiar--things such as money, time, words, emotions, sex, and food. Food? Is food a problem area for you? It could be.

We all need food. We all love to eat; it is a critical part of our humanity. When I'm congested from a head cold and lose my taste for a few days, I feel subhuman. Yes, we all can be tempted by food, in one fashion or another. Therefore, how we handle the power of food is a wisdom issue. "The earth . . . cannot bear up: under . . . a fool when he is satisfied with food" (Prov. 30:21-22). Satisfying the appetite is so critical to loving God that we are wise to pray: "Feed me with the food that is my portion, that I not be full and deny You and say, 'Who is the Lord?' or that I not be in want and steal, and profane the name of my God" (Prov. 30:8-9). What do we need to know about eating to avoid stumbling over food?

(I am indebted for many ideas that follow to Elyse Fitzpatrick, *The Journal of Biblical Counseling*, Vol. XII, No. 1 [1993].)

1. Don't underestimate the importance of eating.

There is plenty of evidence that eating is important.

a. We all need to eat.

Eating is a good part of God's design. He created food, taste buds, and our digestive system. Food replenishes us physically; we're even weak psychologically without it. Who doesn't get cranky when he or she gets hungry? Jesus taught us to pray, "Give us this day our daily bread" (Matt. 6:11). Proverbs indicates that it is a good thing to have enough "for the food of your household, and sustenance for your maidens" (Prov. 27:27). It says, "He who tills his land will have plenty of food . . ." (Prov. 28:19). The godly woman is commended because she "gives food to her household" (Prov. 31:15). You ought to have enough food to share with the poor and your enemy (Prov. 25:21; 22:9). When Jesus fed the five thousand, all of them had "as much as they wanted," with leftovers (John 6:11-12).

It follows that it is a bad thing not to have enough food for your family. "If anyone does not provide for his own, and especially for those of his household, he has denied the faith and is worse than an unbeliever" (1 Tim. 5:8).

b. We spend a lot of time and energy preparing, consuming, and cleaning up after eating.

We might be tempted to view the apparent vanity of it, "All a man's labor is for his mouth and yet the appetite is not satisfied" (Eccl. 6:7), unless Paul had assured us in 1 Corinthians 10:31: "Whether, then, you eat or drink or whatever you do, do all to the glory of God."

c. Hunger is a motivator to work.

"A worker's appetite works for him" (Prov. 16:26).

"If anyone is not willing to work, then he is not to eat,

either" (2 Thess. 3:10).

d. The first sin on earth involved eating.

In Genesis 2:9, God gave Adam and Eve every tree that is pleasing to the sight and good for food. That's paradise. God told them not to eat from one of the trees (Gen. 2:16-17). Therefore, eating plays some kind of vital role in trusting God and depending on His love. The woman saw the food, ate, and died. The curse that followed cites eating as a part of their sin, and connects a newly cursed ground to eating for the rest of their lives: " 'Because you . . . have eaten from the tree about which I commanded you . . . cursed is the ground because of you; in toil you will eat of it all the days of your life" (Gen. 3:17).

e. Feasting is important to God

"Three times a year you shall celebrate a feast to Me" (Ex. 23:14).

God delighted to give His people "a land where you will eat food without scarcity" (Deut. 8:7-9). In the parable of the prodigal son (Luke 15), the father (representing God) calls for a feast to kill the fattened calf in order to celebrate the return of His lost son. Jesus participated in enough feasts to be labeled a glutton by His enemies (Matt. 11:19).

f. Overeating is condemned by God.

"The glutton will come to poverty" (Prov. 23:21).

"Have you found honey? Eat only what you need" (Prov. 25:16).

"He who is a companion of gluttons humiliates his father" (Prov. 28:7).

It must also be true that starving ourselves to death is a sin, since God alone has ultimate rights over our bodies.

g. Eating enhances relationships.

God Himself ordains covenant making and renewal ceremonies to be accompanied by eating. The Lord's Table is a covenant meal. We eat in the presence of the Lord, after the pattern of Jesus eating with the disciples the covenant meal remembering the Passover. After the resurrection, Jesus had fellowship with His disciples around a meal. He prepared a breakfast of fish and bread for them (John 21:9-13).

Apparently the disciples got the message because they regularly met together to break bread (Acts 2:46) and for the agape feasts (1 Cor. 11:17ff). Eating appropriately fosters corporate and intimate relationships. There's something right about a romantic candlelight dinner for intimacy. There's something right about Norman Rockwell's painting of Thanksgiving dinner.

2. Eating is a mirror on your heart.

a. It pictures what is important to you.

If your attitude is: I can eat whatever I want whenever I want, perhaps you have a proud, independent spirit. If your attitude is: I probably shouldn't have another piece of chocolate cake but I really feel overwhelmed with life and it will make me feel better, maybe you have a self-pitying spirit. If you have a serious eating disorder such as bulimia or anorexia, perhaps it indicates you have a controlling spirit.

If you have no intention to stop to bless your food, perhaps you have an ungrateful heart. If you usually bless your food at home but won't in public perhaps it reveals your reputation is more important to you than piety, or that you fear man.

The Lord Jesus, after a forty-day fast, was tempted by the devil with matters of ultimate importance: Why not turn those stones to bread? Jesus, however, believed that "man shall not live on bread alone, but on every word that proceeds out of the mouth of God" (Matt. 4:4). In contrast, Esau sold his birthright to his brother Jacob in exchange for some of Jacob's lentil stew, simply to satisfy his appetite (Gen. 25:34). Hebrews 12:15-17 comments on Esau's inability to repent: his stomach seared his conscience. We see that food is powerful and able to control us. We can easily crave it (1 Cor. 10:5-7).

b. Eating exposes a demanding spirit.

Have you ever said, I want dinner NOW! Why isn't there ANY milk in the house? The service in this restaurant is atrocious! I only go to the best restaurants in town. We find examples in the Bible of demanding. In 1 Corinthians 11:20-22, Paul rebukes the church because when they met for the agape meal the rich wouldn't wait for the poor to arrive and consumed their food ahead of time. "For in your eating each one takes his own supper first; and one is hungry and another is drunk" (1 Cor. 11:21). In Psalm 78:17-20, Asaph laments that Israel was filled with unbelief and sarcasm, "He struck the rock so that waters gushed out . . . . Can [God] give bread also? Will He provide meat for His people?" Exodus 16:2 reports, "The whole congregation of the sons of Israel grumbled . . . . 'Would that we had died by the Lord's hand in the land of Egypt when we sat by pots of meat, when we ate bread to the full . . . ' ". They wanted to go back to Egypt to eat!

How are you tempted to turn back to Egypt?

How do you respond to fear, anxiety, uncertainty, or pressure? God desires to free your heart from trusting in the arm of the flesh as well as the flesh that strengthens the arm. Has food impaired your ability to be a leader in your home? Have you missed ministry opportunities because of eating? God will test your heart via your stomach: "And He humbled you and let you be hungry, and fed you with manna which you did not know, nor did your fathers know, that He might make you understand that man does not live by bread alone, but man lives by everything that proceeds out of the mouth of the Lord" (Deut. 8:2-3).

c. Eating exposes your ultimate satisfier.

How do you determine whether food has an ultimate grip on your heart? Through fasting. I'm not sure we can ultimately enjoy food until we're free to fast from it. How does God teach us about self-control until we're tempted to lose it? The Bible shows numerous instances when the Lord is sought in a special way through fasting (Ps.35:13; Ezra 8:21; Acts 13:2; Joel 2:12; Matt.9:14-15). The times I've fasted I realize how a tiny thing like a candy bar can tempt me. Does mere hunger pain cause you to ignore God's commands to patience, peace, and thankfulness? Heed the warning of Philippians 3:19 for those "whose end is destruction, whose god is their appetite . . . who set their minds on earthly things."

What ultimately satisfies your heart? Is Christ alone your comfort and savior? Jesus said, "Do not work for the food which perishes, but for the food which endures to eternal life, which the Son of Man will give to you . . . . For the bread of God is that which comes down out of heaven . . . . 'I am the bread of life . . . ' " (John 6:27ff). Do you see? Food is for the stomach. The stomach can be a pathway to the heart. Notice the connection between heart and food in Isaiah 55:1-2: "Ho!

216

Every one who thirsts, come to the waters; and you who have no money come, buy and eat. Come, buy wine and milk without money and without cost. 'Why do you spend your money for what is not bread, and your wages for what does not satisfy? Listen carefully to Me, and eat what is good, and delight yourself in abundance."

This text asks you a profound question: Is the abundance for which you are spending your life satisfying you? Are you settling for spiritual junk food or counterfeits? There is a reason spiritual counterfeits leave you empty. Lack of satisfaction should lead you to the place where you can buy without money. Only at that place God Himself provides the manna of eternal grace through His Son--at the cross. What was expensive to Jesus is for us a storehouse of unending paradise. In order to buy from God salvation and paradise, you have to know you have nothing. Your poverty is your wealth.

Nothing in my hands I bring, simply to thy cross I cling.

Naked come to thee for dress, helpless look to thee for grace, foul I to the fountain fly, wash me savior, or I die.

(Augustus Toplady)

God shows us our helplessness spiritually in the fact that we continue to hunger after we eat. As good as any food is, it can't keep us forever. Your good works may be wonderful things, but they can't keep you forever. What can you trust that will keep you forever? There's one thing--the righteous life and sacrificial death of Jesus Christ. He is the bread of life. If you have Him by faith, you have eternal life.

3. Eating is a foretaste of eternity.

There is something sensual about eating. It pleases the

palate, soothes the soul, and bolsters the body. Christians eat at the Lord's Table—rather than touch a special object such as a cross, or chant a special prayer--because God wants them to be reminded of two concrete historical realities that are easy to forget.

First, as real as the communion elements are, so real is Christ's death for their sins. Taste the bread, savor the wine, think about His body and blood, the body into which your sins were nailed once for all, and the blood that God accepts as having cleansed you in an instant, for all time, of all the pollution of your sin. Savor His forgiving grace.

Second, the ultimate meal is the marriage supper of the lamb (Rev. 19), an indescribable celebration of eternal scope. We can taste it now. As real as this food is, so real will be the smell, touch, taste of indestructible life, paradise, and existence without sin, sickness or sorrow, in the presence of God in Jesus.

The Fruit of the Vine

So your barns will be filled with plenty
and your vats will overflow with new wine. (Prov. 3:10)

Wine is a mocker, strong drink a brawler,
and whoever is intoxicated by it is not wise. (Prov. 20:1)

Is alcohol a stumbling block along the path of life? Most definitely. It is today as it was in ancient times. What should our attitude be toward the fruit of the vine? Should we stay away completely because of its potential dangers, leaving untouched one of God's gifts to His creatures? Or is there a way to enjoy potentially harmful drink without actually sinning? Christians have not agreed on the answer to this question. To find ours, a good place to start is the Garden of Gethsemane. We hear Jesus in prayer. He is in agony. If there ever was a dark night of the soul, this is it.

Jesus instituted the Last Supper with His disciples in the upper room and walked roughly a mile across the Kidron Valley east of Jerusalem to an olive grove. He told his faithful followers to wait and pray. Jesus has arrived at His anticipated horrific earthly end. His short 33 years on earth will conclude in torment at 3:00 p.m. the next day following hours of torture. He is on the verge of experiencing sorrow, shame, bitterness, torment of soul, unspeakable physical pain, and immeasurable psychological devastation. Humanly, it is too much. Thus Jesus prays,

"My Father, if it is possible, let this cup pass from me; yet not as I will, but as you will" (Matt. 26:39).

All that Jesus is about to suffer is represented or symbolized in the cup. We need to explore the cup with three questions:

1.   What is the cup?

There are two other allusions to Jesus' cup in the NT:

"Jesus therefore said to Peter, 'Put the sword into the sheathe; the cup which the Father has given me, shall I not drink it?'" (John 18:11).

"Are you able to drink the cup I am about to drink?" (Matt. 20:22).

Because these alone don't tell us enough, we need to know what is in the cup that makes it so terrifying. To determine that we examine two different cups in the OT:

a. The cup of blessing

"My cup overflows" (Ps. 23:5).

"The Lord is the portion of my inheritance and my cup" (Ps. 16:5).

"I shall lift up the cup of salvation, and call upon the name of the Lord" (Ps. 116:13).

This cup is a metaphor for God's provision. We drink in God's goodness.

"They drink their fill of the abundance of Your house; and You give them to drink of the river of Your delights" (Ps. 36:8).

b. The cup of cursing (a much more prominent use of "cup" in the OT)

"Upon the wicked He will rain snares; fire and brimstone and burning wind will be the portion of their cup" (Ps. 11:6).

"And let him drink of the wrath of the Almighty" (Job 21:20).

"All the nations will drink continually. They will drink and swallow and become as if they had never existed" (Obad. 16).

"For thus the Lord, the God of Israel says to me, 'Take this cup of the wine of wrath from my hand and cause all the nations to whom I send you to drink it'" (Jer. 25:15, cf. 17, 28).

"For a cup is in the hand of the Lord, and the wine foams; it is well mixed, and he pours out of this. Surely all the wicked of the earth must drain and drink down its dregs" (Ps. 75:8).

You notice in these allusions that wine is in the cup. It is a metaphor of the Lord's anger or fury. Why wine and not oil or water or a vegetable juice or honey? Wine is a perfect metaphor because it represents both God's blessing and wrath. Wine can be either sweet or bitter; it can cheer or mock; it can be smooth or biting.

Wine is symbolic of blessings:

"He will love you and bless you and multiply you; he will also bless the fruit of your womb and the fruit of your ground, your grain and your new wine and your oil, the increase of your herd and the young of your flock, in the land which he swore to your forefathers to give to you" (Deut. 7:13).

"The mountains will drip with sweet wine" (Joel 3:18).

"The Lord of hosts will prepare a lavish banquet for all peoples on this mountain; a banquet of aged wine, choice pieces with marrow, and refined, aged wine" (Isa. 25:6).

"You have put gladness in my heart, more than when their grain and new wine abound" (Ps. 4:7).

"He causes the grass to grow for the cattle, and vegetation for the labor of man, so that he may bring forth food from the earth, and wine which makes man's heart glad" (Ps. 104:14-15).

"May God give you . . . an abundance of grain and new wine" (Gen. 27:28).

"And Melchizedek king of Salem brought out bread and wine; now he was a priest of God Most High" (Gen. 14:18).

"Men prepare a meal for enjoyment, and wine makes life merry" (Eccl. 10:19).

"Go then, eat your bread in happiness and drink your wine with a cheerful heart; for God has already approved your works" (Eccl. 9:7).

"Ephraim will be like a mighty man, and their heart will be glad as if from wine . . . " (Zech. 10:7).

"May he kiss me with the kisses of his mouth! For your love is better than wine" (Song 1:2).

"I have come into my garden, my sister . . . I have eaten my honeycomb and my honey; I have drunk my wine and my milk" (Song 5:1).

The fact that wine is celebrated means that, far from being forbidden in the OT, or even merely tolerated, wine is a drink of choice.

It is important to note that in Hebrew (new) wine is distinguished from grape juice. According to Numbers 6:3, a Nazirite "shall abstain from wine (yayin) and strong drink (shekar); he shall drink no vinegar, whether made from wine or strong drink, nor shall he drink any grape juice (enab mishrah) . . . . " The clear implication is that anyone who has not taken this vow may enjoy these things.

Wine is symbolic of cursing or judgment:

"Your silver has become dross, your drink diluted with water" (Isa. 1:22).

"Thus says the Lord God, 'You will drink your sister's cup, which is deep and wide. You will be laughed at and held in derision; it contains much. You will be filled with drunkenness and sorrow, the cup of horror and desolation . . .' " (Ezek. 23:32-33).

"I trod down the peoples in my anger and made them drunk in my wrath, and I poured out their lifeblood on the earth" (Isa. 63:6).

"You have made Your people experience hardship; you have given us wine to drink that makes us stagger" (Ps. 60:3),

"Rouse yourself! . . . you who have drunk from the Lord's hand the cup of his anger, the chalice of reeling you have drained to the dregs" (Isa. 51:17, cf. 22).

"Babylon has been a golden cup in the hand of the Lord, intoxicating all the earth. The nations have drunk of her wine; therefore the nations are going mad" (Jer. 51:7).

"He [who worships the beast] also will drink of the wine of the wrath of God, which is mixed in full strength in the cup of His anger; and he will be tormented with fire and brimstone in the presence of the holy angels and in the presence of the Lamb" (Rev. 14:10).

"Babylon the great was remembered before God, to give her the cup of the wine of His fierce wrath" (Rev. 16:19).

God is making people drunk. Not literally, but figuratively. Why this image? Why not crippling, blinding, drowning, losing hair, or eating manure?

a. As we've just seen, it is appropriate because wine symbolizes both curse and blessing.

b. Just as the abuse of wine produces intoxication, so the abuse of any good gift produces sin. God says that spiritual idolatry is harlotry or adultery.

c. Sin is as dehumanizing as drunkenness. Sin takes us out of our good senses as does drunkenness. "Harlotry, wine [yayin] and new wine [tirosh] take away the understanding [heart]" (Hos. 4:11). People choose to sin even as they choose to get drunk; therefore, the soul that chooses sin over God is as foolish as a drunk.

d. Drunkenness is, therefore, a picture of intoxication with sin. Nothing could be more dehumanizing. Unforgiven sin will incur God's wrath, because sin inflames His heart to judgment. When we drink of God's wrath in judgment we experience the ultimate disintegration of our humanity. We weren't made for sin or judgment!

Notice God doesn't say wine itself is bad. It is the abuse of wine that's bad. Jesus said, "There is nothing outside the man which can defile him if it goes into him" (Mark 7:15).

God offers us wine:

"Ho! Everyone who thirsts, come to the waters; and you who have no money come, buy and eat. Come, buy wine and milk without money and without cost" (Isa. 55:1).

"Wisdom has built her house, she has hewn out her seven pillars; she has prepared her food, she has mixed her wine" (Prov. 9:1-2).

"You may spend the money for whatever your heart desires: for oxen, or sheep, or wine [yayin], or strong drink [shekar], or whatever your heart desires; and there you shall eat in the presence of the Lord your God and rejoice, you and your household" (Deut. 14:26).

God commands wine as an offering to Him:

"And there shall be one-tenth of an ephah of fine flour mixed with one-fourth of a hin of beaten oil, and one-fourth of a hin of wine for a drink offering with one lamb" (Ex. 29:40).

"Pour out a drink offering of strong drink to the Lord" (Num. 28:7).

We have to live with a tension here. God gives something that can be abused; but that's true with many things: authority, sex, sleep, words, food, work, etc. To forbid the use of something God gives is legalism, binding the conscience where God has not. To play it safe and abstain where God has freed us is to have higher ethics than God.

With the tension, understandably, comes a warning: Don't be intoxicated by any of these. The Bible warns against slavery to alcohol:

"Woe to those who rise early in the morning that they may pursue strong drink, who stay up late in the evening that wine may inflame them!" (Isa. 5:11).

Scripture equally condemns drunkenness:

" . . . nor thieves, nor the covetous, nor drunkards, nor revilers, nor swindlers, will inherit the kingdom of God" (1 Cor. 6:10).

"Do not get drunk with wine, for that is dissipation, but be filled with the Spirit . . . " (Eph. 5:18).

"Wine is a mocker, strong drink a brawler, and whoever is intoxicated by it is not wise" (Prov. 20:1).

This verse seems to indicate that the drunk is mocked by wine, "Look at you, acting like a fool!" As a brawler, strong drink starts a fight in the heart, a conflict between righteous and unrighteous desires in which the drunk invariably gives in to his lustful passions.

Notice that this verse makes the quantity of wine consumed a wisdom issue. So is the circumstance under which wine is used:

"Who has woe? Who has sorrow? . . . Those who linger long over wine . . . " (Prov. 23:29-30).

"Do not be with heavy drinkers of wine . . . " (Prov. 23:20).

"It is not for kings to drink wine . . . for they will drink and forget what is decreed . . . " (Prov. 31:4),

"Do not drink wine or strong drink . . . when you come into the tent of meeting, so that you will not die . . . " (Lev. 10:9).

Notice that in each of the above verses wine drinking itself is assumed and not unlawful; by implication you are free to use wine under other circumstances.

A distinction was made between Jesus and John the Baptist; John took a vow of poverty and abstinence, while Jesus did not—and was accused of being a drunk. "The Son of Man came eating and drinking, and they say, 'Behold, a gluttonous man and a drunkard . . . " (Matt. 11:19).

The issue with how we use God's blessings is always the heart. From the heart flow all sins (Mark 7:14-23).

The Old Testament indicates it can be safe to use alcohol in moderation, but does the New Testament? Some try to argue that the wine mentioned in the New Testament is grape juice, or wine diluted four times with water. If so, the connection between wine and drunkenness makes no sense. Sometimes wine was watered down to improve taste; nevertheless, warnings against drunkenness clearly imply it was potent enough to cause inebriation.

Some examples:

a. First Timothy 3:8 warns that a church officer should not be "addicted to much wine." How could anyone be addicted to it if it's so watered down?

b. In Acts 2:13 we read that the disciples were mocked and accused of being "full of sweet wine."

c. Paul reports in 1 Corinthians 11:20-21, "When you meet together, it is not to eat the Lord's Supper, for in your eating each one takes his own supper first; and one is hungry and another is drunk." At the agape meal some of the believers are drunk. Why? Because the wine they drank made them so. This tells us that the early church understood that at the Last Supper Jesus used wine.

d. Paul tells Timothy, "use a little wine for the sake of your stomach and your frequent ailments." If that is actually grape juice, why would Paul tell Timothy to drink it, since that's what everyone drank anyway? (1 Tim. 5:23).

e. At the wedding at Cana the wine ran out (John 2:10). "Every man serves the good wine first," Scripture says, but Jesus provides the best wine last, symbolizing that His provisions surpass those of the old covenant.

f. In Romans 14:21 it is the weaker brother, the one whose conscience is not informed as it should be, who stumbles when another drinks wine.

It is worth noting that the Greek word for grape juice (trux) is not used in the NT.

Now let's return to Gethsemane. The cup Jesus drank was full of the fury of His Father's wrath. That's why He didn't want it. In His suffering and at the cross He drank that cup that foamed with the wine of God's wrath for all who trust in Him.

2. Why does Jesus drink it?

He knew exactly what it represented--the bitter wrath of God. It was the only way for Jesus to save His people. Jesus obeyed His Father perfectly: "Not as I will but as You will" (Matt. 26:39). Jesus loved you in doing so. "I lay down my life for the sheep" (John 10:15). He went to the extreme for you. Can you for Him? Because of His deep love you will never taste that wrath! (Romans 8:1).

3. What happened to it?

The cup of cursing Jesus drank was transformed into the cup of blessing, as predicted by Isaiah 25:6-8:

"The Lord of hosts will prepare a lavish banquet for all peoples on this mountain; a banquet of aged wine, choice pieces with marrow, and refined, aged wine. And on this mountain He will swallow up the covering which is over all peoples, even the veil which is stretched over all nations. He will swallow up death for all time, and the Lord God will wipe tears away from all faces, and He will remove the reproach of His people from all the earth . . . . "

"Is not the cup of blessing which we bless a sharing in the blood of Christ?" (1 Cor. 10:16).

Wine is, therefore, used at the Lord's Supper in accordance with the biblical picture of blessing. We're not intoxicated by it, but we are reminded of the intoxicating effect of the gospel. It makes our hearts merry.

A historical note:

The grape juice served at many communion services in America simply doesn't carry the force of the image. Why do churches use grape juice, considering The Baptist Confession of 1689 stipulates the use of wine at the Lord's Supper? It has been the practice of the Christian church universally to use wine at communion until the temperance movement of the late 1800s. Rev. Dr. Robert S. Rayburn explains (in a sermon dated February 25, 2001) that in 1869 Dr. Thomas Welch, a New Jersey dentist and communion steward at the Methodist church, applied the pasteurization process developed by Louis Pasteur to the juice of grapes. He succeeded in producing grape juice, first sold as Dr. Welch's Unfermented Wine in 1890, then later changed to Dr. Welch's Grape Juice. Most of American Christianity was subsequently gripped by the temperance movement and wine disappeared from the Lord's Supper.

Conclusion

Ten Internalized Values of a Wise Person

The wise will inherit honor,

but fools display dishonor. (Prov. 3:35)

As we conclude this study on the stumbling blocks frequently found on the path of life, it's an appropriate time to ask the question, How do we know if we learned anything? Should we take a final exam? Is Proverbs like a school education? Schools test what you know. You study hard for exams, cram in the data, but then realize not too long after the exam that you have forgotten what you were supposed to learn. Proverbs is about education, in the truest sense of the word. To educate comes from Latin *educare*, which means "to lead out." If the purpose of education is to lead you out of ignorance, out of what does wisdom lead us?

Wisdom leads us out of foolishness. It leads us out of thinking we have the answers within ourselves, to placing all our confidence in God. If schools test what you know, wisdom tests what you are becoming. The goal of Proverbs is not to make you a person who can rattle off a bunch of spiritual facts–the demons can do that–but to make you a wise person. Wisdom is what you become; you become a wise person. Wisdom is internalized, shaping your being or character. It isn't merely a matter of making a wise decision when the opportunity presents itself, but living, thinking, and processing life wisely.

So, what does a person who has assimilated wisdom's values look like? If Proverbs presents itself as a parent instructing a son, what should you see in your child at the end point of your parenting? What core values should be pulsating through your heart if wisdom has impacted you?

Let's review the ten values that tend to leap off the page at us from Proverbs.

1. Absolutes

All values come from God.

"Trust in the Lord with all your heart and do not lean on your own understanding, in all your ways acknowledge Him, and He will make your paths straight" (Prov. 3:5-6).

"The fear of the Lord is the beginning of wisdom, and the knowledge of the Holy One is understanding" (Prov. 9:10).

Trusting and fearing the Lord are the lens through which you see the world. It is inescapable that everyone has some lens. The biblical lens makes perfectly good sense. Life began with God; therefore, life is only understood on God's terms. Since He is the moral king and judge of the universe, all values come from Him. If He says something is good, then it is good, and always will be. If He says something is wrong, then it is wrong, and always will be, unless He changes it. Teach your children that we don't live by feelings, impressions, or man-made opinions, but by truth. Truth is in the Word of God, and everything in God's creation can only ultimately be understood in relation to His self-revelation in the Bible. Life has a wonderful designer. We enjoy life only to the degree that we live and move in conformity to the designer's plan. How would we apply that to culture? We teach our children not to bury their heads from it, nor to be absorbed by it, but to observe it from God's perspective so they can be agents of renewal in it.

2. Stewardship

All possessions come from God.

"Honor the Lord from your wealth and from the first of all your produce" (Prov. 3:9).

There is nothing you have--health, intelligence, good experiences--that isn't a gift from the hand of God. It's all on loan from a gracious provider who always wants us to enjoy what we have, but never to be possessed by it. That means you will learn to challenge yourself. Which do you cherish most, all the good things God gives, or the Giver of all good things?

Wisdom also instructs us that the first question asked about stewardship is not, How much should I give? Rather, What does God own? Then secondly, How do I live as a faithful steward—caring for what belongs to God that has been entrusted to my care--in a world with enormous survival and spiritual needs? Once you ask the right questions, you will be intentional, serious, and sacrificial in your giving to the kingdom of Christ. You will pray for opportunities to give. You will be marked by humble gratitude. You will be fooled less by American consumerism, which says you deserve the best and the newest. You don't think you're fooled? Do you pray for the gift of giving? When did you last confess greed to another person? We don't confess it because we don't see it in ourselves.

3. Motives

All activity is to be done for God's glory.

"The fear of the Lord is to hate evil; pride and arrogance and the evil way and the perverted mouth, I hate" (Prov. 8:13).

The fear of the Lord is the operational principle of everything a wise person does; his motive is the glory of God. "Whether, then, you eat or drink or whatever you do, do all to the glory of God" (1 Cor. 10:31).

Two motives that especially snag us are pride and fear. Fear of doing wrong, pride in doing well. Nothing in life is pointless. Because we were made by God for His glory, His pleasure should be the motive for all we do.

4. Dependence

All of life is dependent on God.

"Turn to my reproof, behold, I will pour out my spirit on you; I will make my words known to you" (Prov. 1:23).

God is the source of every breath we take. He is the giver of life. God delights when we express our dependence on Him in prayer. How and why and when you pray are the sure measures of your sense of dependence on God.

5. Humility

All of our worth is borrowed from God.

"When pride comes, then comes dishonor, but with the humble is wisdom" (Prov. 11:2).

Teach your children to think of God before themselves. Humility is not thinking less of yourself, but thinking of yourself less. The humble know they are self-centered, and lean hard against it. Humility can be measured by the way people speak. Are they too often giving their own opinions? Do they need to prove something? Are they combative and

234

argumentative? Do they use words as a commodity to promote the welfare of others?

6. Praise

We were created to worship God.

"Nothing you desire compares with me" (Prov. 3:15, 8:11).

Teach your children why worship is vital to all of life. We offer personal acts of worship six days a week so we can bring our "worship collateral" with us to corporate worship. What core truth primes the pump of heart worship?

"One generation shall praise Your works to another, and shall declare Your mighty acts" (Ps. 145:4).

That means those of us who have lived longer than the youth have a privilege and responsibility to tell them how worthy God is of our devotion, and that it is worth everything to follow Jesus.

7. Conviction

We are sinners in need of a savior.

"Who can say, 'I have cleansed my heart, I am pure from my sin?'" (Prov. 20:9).

Notice how this talks about sin as a heart issue, not simply behaviors. Sin is an attitude of self-centeredness that expresses itself in behavior. Conviction means taking responsibility for sin. Psychologists have coined a new disorder: intermittent explosive disorder. It's a new term for road rage. The Bible calls it losing self-control, anger, sin. The evidence that you take sin seriously is your willingness to receive correction or reproof. "Whoever loves discipline loves knowledge, but he who hates reproof is stupid" (Prov. 12:1).

8. Inquiry

We are called to think God's thoughts.

"Acquire wisdom! Acquire understanding! . . . The beginning of wisdom is: acquire wisdom; and with all your acquiring, get understanding" (Prov. 4:5-8).

We don't do inquiry for its own sake, but toward the goal of understanding the majesty of how God has wired the universe. We do inquiry using the precious tool of asking questions. I developed a friendship with a retiree in Texas named Fred. He had been an elder in my denomination and chose to attend our church. He loved theology and church history. We met weekly, and each visit he had something to share about a subject he was exploring. Even toward the end of his life, when he was confined to a wheelchair and quite frail, my octogenarian friend had in front of him articles and books from which he was seeking to understand something new about God's Word, theology, or history.

9. Fruitfulness

We are to produce for God.

"He who tills his land will have plenty of bread, but he who pursues worthless things lacks sense"

"The wicked desires the booty of evil men, but the root of the righteous yields fruit"

"A lazy man does not roast his prey, but the precious

possession of a man is diligence" (Prov. 12:11, 12, 27).

Is the main direction of your life self-centered? Are you submitting to God in prayer those things you desire, asking Him to confirm what will prove to be the best use of your time and talents? Years ago I began to feel as if I might be peaking in my pickup basketball career. I returned home after a good outing one day and told my wife, "Honey, I'm not getting any younger. If I'm ever going to dunk a basketball, it's now. I've decided to work extra hard on strengthening my legs and vertical jump so I can dunk." I anticipated her replying, "Oh dearest one, so athletic and talented, what a brilliant idea. I think the time is now or never. Go for it! And I'll be there to cheer you on when you dunk for the first time in a game."

Well, she didn't quite respond as I had hoped. She simply said, in as nice a way as possible, "Don't you think you have more important things to work on than that?" She was right, as usual, my blessed voice of wisdom. So I've never dunked in a basketball game in my entire life . . . and that's just fine.

I'm not saying you shouldn't pursue whatever dunking is for you. I'm encouraging you to submit that to God in prayer, as you pray for the needs of others in your family, community, and world, and ask God for direction. Ask Him to show you how to bear fruit that will be enduring. What inspires me is good stewards such as my friend Tom. He pastored a congregation in my denomination in a lovely city in my state, with a wonderful ministry to a nearby university. He grew the leadership and budget, leading the church into an attractive new building. From my perspective that is the kind of place in which you sail into retirement. Not Tom. After prayer, seeking wisdom from friends, and honest dialogue, he left his calling there as pastor of the church to become an associate pastor in a good friend's church in Tennessee. Why give up weekly preaching and the high privilege of leading the flock? For Tom, it was a matter of using his gifts for the greatest impact in God's kingdom for his last decade of ministry. He possessed a gift mix his friend needs, and as an act of faithful stewardship he packed up and ventured out.

Before we come to the last one, we must point out that none of these things qualifies you for heaven. These are marks of a changed heart, not a restrained heart. Without a new heart they will merely be like decorations on a cut Christmas tree . . . in June! Even with a new heart you'll never do any of these perfectly this side of heaven. Our best efforts are tainted with sin. That's why the most important value is our last,

10. Grace

God loves us in spite of our performance.

"Though He scoffs at the scoffers, yet He gives grace to the afflicted" (Prov. 3:34).

God offers abundant salvation grace to those afflicted by sin, through faith in Jesus' life and death. This grace fits us for heaven, and sustains us through afflictions. It is often in affliction, when all other things are stripped away, that we find out whether the other nine qualities have been internalized.

Thou lovely source of true delight,

Whom I unseen adore,

Unveil thy beauties to my sight,

That I might love thee more.

Oh that I might love thee more.

What kind of person would write lyrics like that? A person who has these qualities pulsating through her soul. A person

238

who knows God's grace in salvation and in affliction. Anne Steele wrote those lyrics, plus hundreds of others.

Kevin Twit, contemporary songwriter, explains her story. She lived in England from 1716-1778. She was born in Broughton, where her father was a timber merchant and preached at the Baptist church for sixty years--most of the time without receiving a salary. Her mother died when she was three years old, and when she was 19 she suffered a severe injury to her hip, rendering her an invalid for most of her life. When she was 21, she was engaged to Robert Elscourt, but the day before the wedding he was drowned while bathing in a river. She was never married, and assisted her father in his pastoral labors for her whole life. She lost her mobility the last nine years of her life, and was never able to leave her bed. In spite of all this, her disposition was described as cheerful and helpful and her life as one of unaffected humility, warm benevolence, sincere friendship, and genuine devotion.

Jesus, my Lord, my Life, my Light,

O come with blissful ray,

Break radiant through the shades of night,

And chase my fears away,

Won't you chase my fears away.

—*Anne Steele*

SCRIPTURE INDEX

About the Author

Mike Sharrett graduated from Gettysburg College (BA Philosophy) in 1978 and received an MEd from the University of Virginia (Counselor Education) in 1979. He joined the University of Virginia faculty as an assistant director in the Office of Career Planning and Placement, counseling students and teaching an undergraduate course in career planning. Sensing a call to the ministry in 1982, he joined the staff of Trinity PCA in Charlottesville as a lay pastor. In 1985, Mike attended Westminster Theological Seminary in Philadelphia (MDiv) and returned to Trinity as an associate pastor, being ordained in 1988.

In 1992, Mike was called to church planting in Fort Worth, Texas. During twelve years there, he was elected to the board of trustees of Westminster Seminary in Philadelphia and taught several practical theology classes at the Westminster Dallas campus. He also served on the state committee for Reformed University Fellowship, and was delighted to see a strong RUF develop at Texas Christian University in Fort Worth.

Desiring to plant another church, Mike moved to Lynchburg, Virginia, in 2004 to lead a regional church planting movement. His wife of 27 years, Janice, is a teacher in a Christian classical school. They have three children, Mike, Luke, and Laura. Mike enjoys most sports, especially golf and bodysurfing.

Printed in the United States
147185LV00003B/7/P